D1456951

ASIAN CIVILIZATION

This series of interdisciplinary readings is designed to introduce the western reader to the distinctive components of Asian civilization—social order, political institutions, economic problems, and cultural milieu. Each set of paired volumes contrasts ancient and modern subjects; ageless tradition has been balanced by recent analysis to reveal historical continuity amid the unprecedented change occurring in Asia today.

John Bastin, the editor of this volume in the Asian Civilization series, is Reader in the Modern History of Southeast Asia at the School of Oriental and African Studies at the University of London. He was formerly Professor of History at the University of Malaya, and has written and edited several books in the field of Southeast Asian studies.

THE EMERGENCE OF
MODERN SOUTHEAST ASIA:
1511=1957

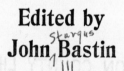

Edited by
John Bastin

Prentice-Hall, Inc. A SPECTRUM BOOK *Englewood Cliffs, N.J.*

Library of Congress Catalog Card Number: 67-14838.

Printed in the United States of America—C.

Current printing (last number):

10 9 8 7 6 5 4 3 2 1

For Jenny

CONTENTS

vii

THE EMERGENCE OF
MODERN SOUTHEAST ASIA:
1511-1957

INTRODUCTION

This book deals with the 450 years of Southeast Asian history that commenced with the arrival of the Portuguese in the Straits of Malacca at the beginning of the sixteenth century and ended with the departure of the Dutch, French, Americans, and British from Indonesia, Indo-China, the Philippines, Burma, and Malaysia after the Second World War. During this period, which has been described in somewhat broader context as the Vasco da Gama epoch of Asian history,[1] all the countries of Southeast Asia, with the notable exception of Thailand, were at one time or another subject to Western rule. The nature of this rule and the means by which it was imposed differed considerably from one part of the region to another and presents the historian of colonialism in Southeast Asia with an extremely variegated pattern for analysis.

Although there were undoubtedly subsidiary factors accounting for early Western penetration into Southeast Asia (especially the religious motive[2]), the overriding consideration was the desire to exploit the economic resources of the area, especially the fine spices of eastern Indonesia. The Portuguese capture of the Muslim sultanate of Malacca in 1511[3] was directed to controlling one of the most important *entrepôts* of the spice trade in Southeast Asia, and the conquest of Manila in 1571 enabled the Spaniards to direct expeditions to the Spice Islands and to exchange, by way of Luzon,

[1] K. M. Panikkar, *Asia and Western Dominance,* Allen & Unwin, Ltd., London, 1953.
[2] Selection 4.
[3] Selection 1.

1

the silver of the New World for the porcelains and silks of the
Orient. The entry of the Dutch and British into Southeast Asian
waters at the end of the sixteenth century was similarly determined
by economic considerations.

The establishment of the Dutch and English East India Companies between 1600 and 1602, especially the former with its
enormous financial resources, represented in certain respects something different from the earlier stage of Iberian imperialism in
Southeast Asia; but extreme caution needs to be shown toward the
recently expressed view that Dutch commercial enterprise in Asia
represented the true beginnings of modern colonialism since the
Dutch were "the first to apply the principle of capital investment
to over-seas ventures" in contradistinction to the "feudal" Portuguese who, motivated by a desire for loot and tribute, had no effect whatever on the long-established pattern of Asian trade.[4] However negatively one may characterize the over-all impact of the
Portuguese in Asia,[5] it is well to remember that during most of the
sixteenth and early seventeenth centuries they monopolized a large
part of the cinnamon trade of Ceylon, acted in Macao as bullion
brokers between Japan and China, and, through their possession of
Malacca, caused an initial diversion of the Muslim trade in the
Straits to Achin, which soon set about its own imperialistic course
in Sumatra and the Malay Peninsula.[6]

Because Portuguese power was firmly established in western India and Ceylon at the beginning of the seventeenth century, the
Dutch and British directed their early attention to Indonesia,
especially western Java, where a lucrative *entrepôt* trade flourished,
and the Moluccas, where spices could be collected at the source of
supply. Conflict between the agents of the East India Companies
led in 1623 to the "Massacre of Amboina," which is commonly believed to have marked the end of British activities in the area but
which has now been shown to have had little permanent effect on
the course of British trade in eastern Indonesia.[7] It was, in fact, not
until the end of the century before the Dutch were able to control

[4] G. Masselman, *The Cradle of Colonialism*, Yale University Press, New
Haven, Conn., London, 1963.
[5] Selection 3.
[6] Selection 2.
[7] Selection 5.

the Moluccan spice trade and drive the British out of Bantam in Java, obliging them to establish new trading bases along the west coast of Sumatra.

The mercantile character of the Dutch and English East India Companies largely determined their relationships with the Southeast Asian powers. The trade of the two Companies was geared initially to providing imports of pepper and fine spices for sale in Europe, and, as the real price of silver was much higher in Asia than it was in Europe, this trade was able to be maintained advantageously on the simple basis of shipping silver to Asian markets from European sources of supply. This, in effect, was how the Dutch and British managed their early commercial ventures in Southeast Asia, and it was partly mercantilist opposition at home that led them to develop other avenues of trade, particularly the intra-Asian trade. It was, in fact, through the "country trade," as it came to be called, that the Dutch and English East India Companies made their greatest impact on Southeast Asia, and it was this trade which led to these basically mercantile organizations becoming increasingly territorial in character. Even so, the local Company officials were warned not to become too involved in Southeast Asian politics, and, in those territories of Java which fell under their sway during the seventeenth and eighteenth centuries, the Dutch preferred to adapt their rule to indigenous forms and to interfere only when absolutely necessary in the affairs of the Javanese regents.[8] In West Sumatra, where the British after 1685 engaged in the forced cultivation of pepper,[9] administration was also adapted to local institutions, although because of the weaker Indonesian political structure a greater measure of direct rule was employed there than in Java.

If the Dutch East India Company in the seventeenth century was the most important agency of Western colonialism in Southeast Asia, it was, by the second half of the eighteenth century, unable to compete with the expanding resources of the British in India which enabled the English Company to sustain the lucrative tea trade with China. The failure of the Dutch East India Company to adapt itself to the changing needs of the country trade in Asia was prob-

[8] Selection 7.
[9] Selection 6.

ably of greater significance in accounting for its decline and abolition at the end of the century than was the inefficiency and corruption of its administration; but essentially the Company's ex-
haustion was a reflection of the growing maritime and financial im-
potence of the Netherlands itself at this period. The Company was
formally dissolved at the end of 1799 and its assets taken over by the
Batavian Republic. During the Napoleonic Wars British power in
Southeast Asia was in the ascendant. Java and its dependencies
were captured and ruled for a period of five years (1811 to 1816)
on principles different from those which obtained under the Dutch
East India Company,[10] but after continuing this new system of the
British for a brief period the Dutch reverted to some of the older
principles of administration in 1830 when the Culture System was
introduced.[11] Whatever the defects of this system,[12] it returned
large financial surpluses to the Netherlands.

While the Dutch were commencing their systematic exploitation
of the economic resources of Indonesia, the British were impelled
to extend their imperial boundaries in Southeast Asia. The Treaty
of London (1824)[13] established separate spheres of influence between the two powers, leaving the Dutch with those territories
south of the Straits of Singapore and the British with Singapore itself, Malacca, and the island of Penang off the Malay Peninsula.
However reluctant Great Britain may have been to extend her
commitments in Southeast Asia at this period, she was drawn into
wars with Burma in 1824 to 1826, 1852, and 1885, which led to the
division of the Burmese kingdom and its gradual incorporation
into the British *Raj*.[14] Moreover, in 1874 fear of foreign intervention led Great Britain to undertake the protection and direct the
administration of some of the states of the Malay Peninsula.[15] At
the same time France was pushing her frontiers forward in Indo-
China, the Dutch were attempting to impose their rule over north
Sumatra, and the United States, after war with Spain, assumed

[10] Selection 9.
[11] Selection 10.
[12] Selection 11.
[13] Selection 12.
[14] Selection 13.
[15] Selection 14.

sovereignty in the Philippines. By the end of the nineteenth century the colonial map of Southeast Asia was largely drawn.

The systems of administration which the Western powers adopted in their Southeast Asian dependencies during the twentieth century were based on different principles and different circumstances.[16] French assimilationist policies in Indo-China contrasted with the paternalistic "adjustment-rule" concepts of the Dutch in Indonesia and with the rather conservative ideas of the British in the Malay States; but whatever the form of colonial rule, even when it promised to be of limited duration,[17] there was no ignoring the rising tide of Southeast Asian nationalism with its demand for political independence. In some Southeast Asian countries the nationalist movements were well organized and developed; in others, notably Malaya, nationalist feeling was largely embryonic.[18] The repressive policies of the colonial governments, especially those of the Dutch and French, who acted against the nationalists of Indonesia and Indo-China with great severity,[19] might well have contained the pressures for independence for many years had not the Japanese conquest and occupation of Southeast Asia between 1941 and 1945[20] unleashed forces which made it impossible for the Western governments in 1945 to return to the former state of affairs. Within a little more than a decade after the Second World War, all Southeast Asian countries which had been subject to colonial rule had attained their independence either by revolution, as in the case of Indonesia,[21] or by a process of peaceful devolution of political power, as in the case of Burma and Malaya.[22] Today only part of the island of Timor, still under Portuguese rule, serves as a reminder of the colonial period in Southeast Asia. How this epoch of Asian history is to be assessed is still a matter of violent controversy.[23]

[16] Selections 15-19.
[17] Selection 19.
[18] Selection 20.
[19] Selection 21.
[20] Selections 24 and 25.
[21] Selection 27.
[22] Selection 29.
[23] Selection 30.

1

EARLY WESTERN PENETRATION
INTO SOUTHEAST ASIA

Various impulses lay behind the Portuguese endeavors to find a sea passage to Asia by way of the Cape of Good Hope. Possibly what loomed largest in the early phase of the so-called Age of Discovery was the desire to revive the crusading zeal of Western Christendom following the end of the great Crusades in Syria and Palestine during the thirteenth century. Certainly the bold conception of joining the legendary Christian King Prester John in an anti-Muslim crusade and of outflanking the infidel by sailing around the southern coast of Africa was a major inspiration behind the valiant efforts of Prince Henry the Navigator during the fifteenth century. As those efforts, particularly after Henry's death in 1460, began to be crowned with even more striking success, dreams of Guinea gold and Southeast Asian spices began to loom larger in the minds of the Portuguese captains. Motives inspired by Mammon became, in the words of C. R. Boxer, "inextricably blended with things pertaining to Caesar and to God." It is not without significance that, when the first Portuguese fleet anchored off Calicut in western India in May 1498, one of Vasco da Gama's men, asked by Muslim merchants why the Portuguese had come to Asia, replied that they had come "in search of Christians and of spices."

Spices in large quantities were difficult to find. The spice trade of western India at this period was dominated largely by the Gujerati traders of Cambay, who had agencies in Southeast Asia to which they carried Indian cloths, silks, cottons, and other assorted commodities in exchange for the nutmegs, mace, and cloves of eastern Indonesia. Much of this merchandise was shipped via the great Muslim trading port of Malacca on the Malay Peninsula. It did not take the Portuguese long to realize that, if they wished to eliminate the Gujerati and other Muslim traders from the spice trade, they would have to attempt to seize not only Aden at the entrance to the Red Sea and Ormuz on the Persian Gulf in order to sever the Muslim trade routes, but also Malacca, the *entrepôt* of the spice trade in Southeast Asia.

1. Conquest of Malacca by the Portuguese

The important role played by the sultanate of Malacca in the commerce of South and Southeast Asia at the beginning of the sixteenth century is described in Selection 1 (a) by the contemporary Portuguese chronicler, Duarte Barbosa (The Book of Duarte Barbosa, *translated by M. L. Dames, Hakluyt Society, London, 1918-1921, II, pp. 172-77). Selections (b) and (c) describe the Portuguese conquest of Malacca in 1511 as seen through Portuguese and Malay eyes. [(b) is taken from Tomé Pires'* Suma Oriental *translated and edited by A. Cortesão (Hakluyt Society, London, 1944, II, pp. 287-281), which was written soon after the conquest, and (c) comes from the most important of the early Malay historical works,* Sĕjarah Mĕlayu *(The Malay Annals), which was composed some time before 1536, translated by C. C. Brown (JMBRAS, XXV, 2-3, 1952, pp. 167-169).] All three articles are reprinted by permission.*

(a) Here dwell up to now great wholesale merchants of every kind, both Moors and Heathen, many of them from Charamandel [Coromandel], men of great estates and owning many great ships which they call *juncos* [junks]. They trade everywhere in goods of all kinds. Numbers of ships also come hither to take cargoes of sugar, very fine four-masted ships; they bring great store of silk, very fine raw silk, porcelain in abundance, damasks, brocades, coloured satins, musk, rhubarb, sewing silk in various colours, [much iron], saltpetre, great store of fine silver, pearls in abundance, sorted seed-pearls, gilded coffers, fans, and many other baubles; and all this they sell at good prices to the dealers of the country, and in exchange therefor they take away pepper, incense, Cambay cloths dyed in grain, saffron, coral shaped and strung, and ready for shaping, printed and white cotton cloths which come from Bengala [Bengal], vermilion, quicksilver, opium, and other goods and drugs of Cambaya, and one unknown to us which they call *cacho* and another which they call *pucho mangiçam*, that is gall-nuts brought inland from the Levante to Cambaya by way of Meca, which are much prized in China and Jaoa [Java]. From the Kingdom of Jaoa also come the great *junco* ships [with four masts] to the city of Malaca, which differ much from the fashion of ours, being built of very thick timber, so that when they are old a new planking can be laid over the former . . . and so they remain very strong. The cables and all the shrouds of these ships are made of canes [rattans] which grow in the country. In these ships the Jaos [Javanese] bring hither great store of rice, beef, sheep, swine, deer, "salt meat," fowls, garlic and onions, and also bring for sale many weapons, spears, "daggers," short swords all finely worked and damascened on fine steel . . . and many other small articles . . . and gold which is found in the said Kingdom of Jaoa.

These Jaos who live by sailing the seas take with them their wives and children and homes and families; they have no other houses of their own nor do they ever go ashore save for their traffic, and there in those ships [they are born and there] they die.

These folk, then, selling their goods . . . in Malaca at good prices take away in return cloths of Paleacate [Pulicat] and Mailapur and others which come from Cambaya, opium, rosewater, vermilion, great store of grains for dyeing, raw silk, saltpetre, iron, *cacho* and *pucho* (which are Cambaya drugs) all of which is much valued in Jaoa. From this city of Malaca ships sail also to the Isles of Maluco [Moluccas] . . . there to take in cargoes of cloves, taking thither for sale much Cambaya cloth, cotton and silk of all kinds, other cloths from Paleacate and Bengala, quicksilver, wrought copper, bells and basins, and a Chinese coin . . . pepper, porcelain, garlic, onions, and other Cambaya goods of divers kinds. Thus they sail from this city of Malaca to all the islands in the whole of this sea, and to Timor whence they bring the whole of the white sande[l]s-wood, which is greatly esteemed among the Moors and is worth much; and thither they take iron, axes, knives, cutlasses, swords, cloths from Paleacate [and Cambaya], copper, quicksilver, vermilion, tin, lead, great store of Cambaya beads in exchange wherefor they take away, as well as the sande[l]s-wood, honey, wax and slaves. These ships also sail from Malaca to the islands which they call Bandan [Banda] to get cargoes of nutmegs and mace, taking thither for sale Cambaya goods. They also go to the Island of Çamatra [Sumatra], whence they bring pepper, silk, raw silk, benzoin (great store) and gold, and to other islands bringing thence camphor and aloes-wood; they go to Tenaçary [Tenasserim], Peeguu [Pegu], Bengala, Paleacate, Charamandel, Malabar and Cambaya, so much so that this city of Malaca is the richest seaport with the greatest number of wholesale merchants and abundance of shipping and trade that can be found in the whole world. Gold comes thither in such abundance that the leading merchants dealing in it do not value their estates nor keep their accounts except in *bahares* of gold, which *bahares* are four *quintals* each. . . . There is a certain merchant there who alone will discharge three or four ships laden with every kind of valuable goods and re-lade them alone from his own stock. "They deal also in victuals of various kinds, and all is well paid for and packed. In this city are many foreigners of various lands, who live there and are born in the country; these as I say are Moors with their own distinct language and are called *Malaios* [Malays]." . . . They, "the most distinguished among them," wear short coats which come half way down their thighs of silk, cloth—in grain or brocade—and over this they wear girdles; at their waists they carry daggers in damascene-work which they call *crus* [kĕris]. Their women are "tawny coloured", clad in very fine silk garments and short shirts [decorated with gold and jewels]. "They are very comely, always well-attired, and have very fine hair. . . .

"These Malaios hold the *Alcoram* [Koran] of Mafamede [Muhammad] in great veneration," they have their mosques; they bury their dead; their sons are their heirs; they live in large houses outside the city with many orchards, gardens and tanks, where they lead a pleasant life. They have separate houses for their trade within the city; they possess many slaves with wives and children who live apart and obey all their orders. They are polished and wellbred, fond of music, and given to love.

There are here also merchants [*Chetijs*] of Charamandel who are very corpulent with big bellies, they go bare above the waist, and wear cotton clothes below.

There are also many *Jaos* living here, who are short stunted men with broad ill-formed chests and wide faces; they are Moors, they go naked being clad below the waist in cotton garments whicn they bundle up round them roughly; they wear nothing on their heads and have their hair crisped and standing out on the top [stiff and crisped with care, and some of them shaven]. They are very cunning in every kind of work, skilled in every depth of malice, with very little truth but very stout hearts [and are ready for every kind of wickedness].

(b) Afonso de Albuquerque, Capitan-Major and Governor of the Indies, arrived at Malacca at the beginning of the month of July, in the year 1511, with fifteen sail, great and small, in which came about sixteen hundred fighting men.[1] At this time it is said that Malacca had a hundred thousand men-at-arms, from Kuala Lingi (*Coala Penagy*) to the hinterland (?) and Kasang (*Caçam*), which are the limits of the city of Malacca. And the Malays had many strong palissades, and on the sea there were many lancharas,[2] and *paraos*[2] in the river, and on the sea many junks and Gujarat ships which were ready to fight; because there was then in Malacca a captain from Gujarat who was working for war, as it seemed to him that he alone could cope with our ships and men, all the more because of the immense number of natives, though the natives did not back the king of Malacca; because in trading-lands, where the people are of different nations, these cannot love their king as do natives without admixture of other nations. This is generally the case; and therefore the king was disliked, though his mandarins[3] fought, and that whenever they could.

[1] The figure is in dispute. Albuquerque himself wrote in 1513, "We were in all seven hundred white men and three hundred Malabars. . . ." [ED.]

[2] Malay sailing craft. [ED.]

[3] Malay = *Mĕntĕri*, minister of state. In Malacca there were twenty-eight who collected tribute and exercised various judicial functions. [ED.]

As soon as the said Captain-Major arrived with his fleet, he spent a few days sending messages of peace, trying as much as he could to avoid war. However, the levity of the Malayans, and the reckless vanity and arrogant advice of the Javanese, and the king's presumption and obstinate, luxurious, tyrannical and haughty disposition—because our Lord had ordained that he should pay for the great treason he had committed against our people[4]—all this together made him refuse the desire for peace. They only attempted to delay matters with Malayan messages, strengthening their position as much as they could, as it seemed to them that there was no people in the world powerful enough to destroy them. So the said Governor managed to get back Rui de Araújo and those who were prisoners with him. The king never wanted peace, against the advice of his *Lasamane*[5] and the *Bemdara*[5] and his *Cerina De Raja*[5] that he should make peace; but following his own counsel and that of his son, whom he afterwards killed, and of *Tuam Bandã* and *Tuam Mafamut* and *Utamutarraja* and his son *Pate Acoo,* and the Gujaratees, and *Patiça* and other young nobles who offered to run completely amok for the king, he would hear nothing of peace, the Kashises and their mollahs telling him that he should not make peace; for as India was already in the hands of the Portuguese, Malacca should not pass to the infidels. The king's intention became known, and it was necessary that the said king should not go unpunished for what he did and for the evil counsel he took.

The Governor, having taken counsel, landed with his men and took the city; and the king and his men fled. The Captain-Major returned to the ships that day, and did not allow the said king to be harmed, to see if he would desist from his obstinate intention. The king was unwilling. Finally, the said Governor landed again, determined now to take the city and no longer to be friends with the said king. He took the city and occupied it. The king of Malacca

[4] A reference to the sultan's reception of the first Portuguese mission sent to Malacca in September, 1509. The Malays attempted to kill the Portuguese and seize their ships, but without success. A few Portuguese were captured, however, among them Rui de Araújo who is mentioned in the selection. [ED.]

[5] The great Malay officers of state: *Laksamana* (Admiral), *Běndahara* (Prime Minister and Commander-in-Chief) and [*Tumungo Cerina De Raja* =] *Těměnggong.* [ED.]

fled with his daughters and all his sons-in-law, kings of Kampar and Pahang. They went to *Bretão,* which is the residence of the kings, and the Captain-Major took possession of the city. The city and the sea were cleared up, and authorities were appointed.

The Captain-Major began to make a fortress of wood for want of stone and lime, and in the meantime order was given for the lime; then they began demolishing the wooden one, and they made the famous fortress in the place where it now is, on the site of the great mosque, strong, with two wells of fresh water in the towers, and two or three more in the bulwarks. On one side the sea washes against it, and on the other the river. The walls of the fortress are of great width; as for the keep, where they are usually built, you will find few of five storeys like this. The artillery, both large and small, fires on all sides.

(c) Here now is a story of Fongso [Afonso] d'Albuquerque. At the end of his term of office as viceroy he proceeded to Pertugal and presenting himself before the Raja of Pertugal asked for an armada. The Raja of Pertugal gave him four carracks and five long galleys. He then returned from Pertugal and fitted out a fleet at Goa, consisting of three carracks, eight galeasses, four long galleys and fifteen foysts. There were thus forty (sic) craft in all. With this fleet he sailed for Malaka. And when he reached Malaka, there was great excitement and word was brought to Sultan Ahmad, "The Franks are come to attack us! They have seven carracks, eight galeasses, ten long galleys, fifteen sloops and five foysts." Thereupon Sultan Ahmad had all his forces assembled and he ordered them to make ready their equipment. And the Franks engaged the men of Malaka in battle, and they fired their cannon from their ships so that the cannon balls came like rain. And the noise of the cannon was as the noise of thunder in the heavens and the flashes of fire of their guns were like flashes of lightning in the sky: and the noise of their matchlocks was like that of ground-nuts popping in the frying-pan. So heavy was the gun-fire that the men of Malaka could no longer maintain their position on the shore. The Franks then bore down upon the bridge with their galleys and foysts. Thereupon Sultan Ahmad came forth, mounted on his elephant Jituji. . . .

And the king went forth on the bridge and stood there amid a hail of bullets. But Mukhdam Sadar Jahan clasping the pannier with both hands cried out to Sultan Ahmad Shah[,] "Sultan, this is no place to study the Unity of God, let us go home!" Sultan Ahmad smiled and returned to the palace. And the Franks shouted from their ships, "Take warning, you men of Malaka, to-morrow we land!" And the men of Malaka answered, "Very well!"

Sultan Ahmad Shah then sent out men to assemble all his forces and bid them get ready their arms. . . .

When day dawned, the Franks landed and attacked. And Sultan Ahmad mounted his elephant Juru Demang, with the Sri Awadana on the elephant's head and Tun 'Ali Hati balancing the king on the packsaddle. The Franks then fiercely engaged the men of Malaka in battle and so vehement was their onslaught that the Malaka line was broken, leaving the king on his elephant isolated (?) And the king fought with the Franks pike to pike, and he was wounded in the palm of his hand. And he shewed the palm of his hand, saying "See this, Malays!" And when they saw that Sultan Ahmad was wounded in the hand, the war-chiefs returned to the attack and fought the Franks. . . .

And Malaka fell. The Franks advanced on the king's audience hall(?) and the men of Malaka fled. . . .

Sultan Ahmad then withdrew to Hulu Muar and thence to Pagoh. Sultan Mahmud Shah had taken up his abode at Batu Hampar. Sultan Ahmad then established a fort at Bentayan. Meanwhile the Franks occupied Malaka where they turned the royal demesne into a fort; which fort is there to this day. Then the Franks advanced to Muar and attacked Pagoh, which fell after several days fighting. . . . Sultan Ahmad then withdrew to Hulu Muar. In Muar the Bendahara died: he was buried at Lubok Batu, whereafter he was known at Datok Lubok Batu. After a while Sultan Ahmad and his father, Sultan Mahmud Shah, left Hulu Muar and went on to Pahang, where they were welcomed by the Raja of Pahang. Sultan Mahmud Shah gave his daughter by his Kelantan consort in marriage to the Raja of Pahang whose name was Sultan Mansur Shah. From Pahang Sultan Ahmad went to Bentan and established a settlement at Kopak.

2. *Portuguese Relations with Malaysia and Indonesia*

Tomé Pires, who described Malacca as "a city that was made for merchandise, fitter than any other in the world," believed that a city of such magnitude and wealth could never decline if moderately governed and favored. Moderation was a quality not always to be found in the Portuguese conquerors. Once in possession of this great Southeast Asian entrepôt, they attempted to extend trading privileges to the non-Muslims with the result that, at least initially, many of the long-established Gujerati and other Muslim merchants left the city and began to center their activities on northern Sumatra. Soon a trading conflict developed between Malacca and the north Sumatran sultanate of Achin for possession of the Straits of Malacca. One of the direct effects of Portuguese intrusion into Southeast Asia, in fact, was to stimulate the rise of this sultanate, which commenced an imperialist policy aimed at controlling Pasai and Pedir on Sumatra's east coast and the pepper ports on the west coast. Achin constituted the most serious challenge to the Portuguese in Malacca during the sixteenth and early seventeenth centuries, and the rivalry with this Indonesian state accounts in part, though only in part, for the decline of the great entrepôt of Malacca during this period. The following selection, which examines certain aspects of this subject, is taken from an essay by the late Dutch sociologist B. Schrieke, Indonesian Sociological Studies *(W. van Hoeve, Ltd., The Hague, 1955, I, pp. 42-48). Reprinted by permission.*

After the conquest of Malacca in 1511, the Portuguese in keeping with their principles directed their efforts against the Mohammedans. . . . Closer relations were sought with non-Mohammedan regions such as Sunda (1522) and Panarukan, while within Malacca Hindu traders were given favoured treatment. In the case of the Mohammedans in the town, the Portuguese preferred to do as much injury as possible. The result was an exodus of the Moham-

medan traders, who avoided the usual trade route to the east of
Sumatra and made their way along the west coast of the island,
transferring their *pied à terre* from Malacca to Achin, which then
rapidly developed as a trade centre. Some of the foreign traders
also settled in Bantam in western Java, where within a few years
they succeeded in establishing the power of Islam with the help of
Japara (Demak), thus getting in ahead of the Portuguese before
the latter could reap the profits of their contract with Sunda. From
that time dates the flowering of Bantam and Achin, where the
foreign Mohammedans found their markets. The Portuguese aim
of crippling that trade by striking at its heart in Malacca had
proved in practice to be impossible. In the meantime the old royal
house of Malacca, from which the later rulers of Johore sprang, had
not given up the struggle to reconquer its former territory. A part
of the east coast of Sumatra, the Riau-Lingga Archipelago, and a
section of the peninsula of Malacca were still under its authority.
For Java, too, the possession of Malacca, the trading centre on the
world trade route, was still a goal, just as it was for Achin, which
needed the trade of the Chinese and Javanese. This clash of interests between Java, Johore, and Achin enabled the Portuguese to
maintain their position in Malacca, however much they may have
been harassed at times.

In order to be able to acquire the indispensable Chinese trade,
Achin had to assure itself of the possession of the pepper ports, for
pepper . . . was one of the main products needed by the Chinese. It
is true the Gujarati also had use for a part of it, but it was only a
fairly small amount compared to that taken by the Chinese. Besides petroleum, which they used as a medicine, the Gujarati were
interested in the spices carried from the Moluccas by the Javanese,
camphor from Baros, gold from Minangkabau, tin from Kedah,
and sandalwood from Timor. Aside from those items the chief aim
of their shipping had from early times on been that of carrying on
a barter trade with the Chinese. Now that Malacca was closed to
them they were forced to carry on that trade elsewhere. For Achin
itself as well, the Chinese trade was a vital question—Achin had
need of Chinese pottery, gold, silver, coins, and so forth. This
naturally led to Achinese expansion in the direction of the pepper
ports on Sumatra, Pidië and Pase on the east coast and Priaman

on the west coast. Bantam, where the Chinese also went for pepper, had already made sure of the possession of Selebar in Benkulen and of Lampong for itself.

The expansion of Achin on the east coast of Sumatra inevitably led to a new source of friction with the Portuguese, who for their pepper trade also depended on that area. Since they had to give way to Achin in Pase, they saw themselves forced to obtain their pepper from the ports lying further south—Indragiri, Kampar, and Jambi—with some gold from Minangkabau, the which they were still doing at the beginning of the seventeenth century. . . .

Achin . . . had by the middle of the sixteenth century become the chief station in the intermediary trade of the Mohammedans of western Asia and India with the Indonesian Archipelago—a fact which the Portuguese could only view with eyes of envy. Made strong by its international relations, Achin eventually proved to be invincible to their attacks. . . .

The Portuguese were forced to recognize that their opponents had become too strong for them to be able to enforce their own will by violence. They themselves had been weakened internally by the constant conflict between their personal interests and the king's monopoly, so that after a great number of vain attempts to maintain the artificial monopoly, the basis had to be changed. . . .

It had become more than time for a change of course: not only had the policy followed caused the rise of Achin and Bantam, but even the trade on China had shifted from Malacca to Patani, which was provided with spices from the Moluccas either directly or *via* Johore. A revised toll policy in Malacca brought an improvement, although one tempered by the extortion to which the captains of Malacca often exposed foreign traders. However that may have been, shipping on Malacca increased once more, the Indian Mohammedans also participating in it with a view to obtaining tin. It goes without saying that this had to lead to a decrease in the importance of Achin. Once Malacca thus gradually became the stapling point for the products of the Indies and the point of concentration for trade between China and India once more, it became apparent that . . . they could in such circumstances "leave the Indians free and unencumbered in their trade on the Moluccas, Ambon, and Banda."

For the Javanese, too, it was good business to come to an understanding with the Portuguese. Since their attempts to capture Malacca (in 1513, 1535, 1551, and 1574) had failed and Malacca was nevertheless a necessary market for rice and spices, the Javanese were forced to come to agreement. . . .

The political confusion in the latter half of the sixteenth century [in Java] had not stood in the way of a renewed flowering of trade stimulating the self-confidence of the harbour potentates, however. In fact, the Portuguese after having attempted in vain to monopolize the spices of the Moluccas for themselves had around 1565 had to allow the shipping on the spice islands to go back to the Javanese, whose market area was thus enlarged, even, over what it had earlier been. Malacca's international relations remained highly precarious, however, especially those with Achin and Johore, the two states with which competition in trade was naturally the greatest, so that time and again if conditions seemed good for it there was an attack to be feared. The discord between the surrounding rulers remained Malacca's strength. Peaceful relations were also established with Bantam for some years, for the sake of the pepper trade.

The Portuguese had been forced to give up their monopoly policy in the Moluccas, it is true. They had never had much authority on Banda; the Javanese Mohammedan centre Hitu on Ambon had proved to be too strong for them; and in 1572 they had had to abandon their fort on Ternate. Their effort to achieve exclusive control of the spices had merely been the stimulus for the expansion of the area where cloves were grown—which at their coming had consisted only of Ternate, Tidore, Makian, Batchan, and Motir—, the binding of the inhabitants more closely to Java, and the intensification of Mohammedan activity and pan-Islamic movements, which last found new stimulus in the missionary propaganda of the priests. All this had unloosed forces in the Moluccas the Portuguese were not able to resist. Ternate was presently able to expand to its greatest extent.

In their first years in the East, the Portuguese in order to elude the Javanese had chosen a different route from the customary one (*via* eastern Java, Bali, Bima, and Banda) to the Moluccas, the one *via* northern Borneo. Once there was a Portuguese factory in Grise and a *pied à terre* in Panarukan, however, the traditional trade route was used more frequently again, partly with an eye to the sandalwood trade on Timor and Solor. In the meantime the Malay traders who had fled from Malacca because of the "evil treatment" given them by the captains of the town had settled in Macassar [in the southwest Celebes], where they found a suitable base for shipping on the Moluccas . . . the Macassarese themselves did not carry on any trade worth mentioning, but the place lent itself excellently to being used as a 'chamber of supply' and was at the same time favourably situated as far as the trade on Timor was concerned. Toward the end of the sixteenth century one therefore finds the Portuguese junks usually following this route, to the formation of which the conquest of the extreme east of Java by the Mohammedans contributed its share.

3. The Portuguese Impact on Southeast Asia

The precise influence exercised by the Portuguese in Southeast Asia down to the beginning of the seventeenth century, when their position in the region was challenged by the British and the Dutch, is the subject of considerable debate. This selection, reprinted by permission, from Indonesian Trade and Society *(W. van Hoeve, Ltd., The Hague, 1955, pp. 169-170 and 117-119), by the late Dutch economic historian, J. C. van Leur, emphasizes certain negative aspects of this influence. As Van Leur based most of what he wrote about the Portuguese upon Dutch (that is, biased) sources and made no particular study of Portuguese sources, it is important to contrast this view with the criticism of the book written by Professor C. R. Boxer in* Indonesië *(VIII, 1955, pp. 426-427): Van Leur "repeatedly avers . . . that the Portuguese power in Asia was typically medieval in character, that there was no hierarchy of officials with a distinction between the civil and military power, that Portuguese activities were dominated by lust for plunder and not lust for profit, that they never established an effective commercial monopoly anywhere, and that the Portuguese regime was of little significance commercially or economically. This seems to me to be an exaggeration. The highly organized Indo-Portuguese bureaucracy*

*which flourished at Goa could vie with the elaborate systems of
clerks and officials at Calicut and Hirado which Van Leur so ad-
miringly describes. . . . The Portuguese maintained for over a
century a most effective monopoly of the cinnamon export from
Ceylon, and from 1555 [to] 1609, they skimmed the cream of the
lucrative China-Japan trade."*

The penetration of the Portuguese and the Spanish overseas did
not determine the character of the sixteenth century in southeast
Asia. The Dutch seafarers did not arrive in a Portuguese Asia,
neither a Portuguese India nor a Portuguese Indonesia, but in regions in which the position of the Portuguese was militantly held
in check or repulsed. Portuguese power was typically medieval in
character, a fact which helps to explain its limited effectiveness.
There was not much unity to the scattered territory of port settlements spread out over thousands of miles, despite the centralized
royal shipping from Goa to Europe. There was no hierarchy of officials with a distinction between civil and military administration,
but a conglomeration of nobles and *condottieri* each with his own
retinue of henchmen bound to him by a vassal's loyalty or a lust
for gain; often the officials in authority provided their own equipment and carried out exploitation for their own benefit by means
of offices bestowed on them, frequently on a short term basis. Portuguese power sought its strength, then, not in taking over Oriental
trade or establishing a territorial authority, but in acquiring tribute
and booty. Non-economic motives—lust for plunder, not lust for
profit—played the chief rôle in the overseas expansion. In connection with this the forms for farming out the trade on the Indies, in
which among others the Fuggers and the Welsers had a share, and
for farming out the collection of pepper, forms which meant the
handing over of the most important aspects of commercial exploitation to private persons in exchange for a fixed income, were
characteristic. They were forms typical of political and fiscal capitalism, in which Asian trade and Asian wealth, too, were assigned
their functions anew, for the benefit of the Portuguese authorities'
revenues. . . .
After journeying through the inhospitable seas of southern Africa
the Portuguese ships had come into regions where there was a com-

trade, and authority as highly developed as the
of political capitalism at least as large in dimen-
southern Europe, and probably larger; shipping in
f them carrying more than those used in European
ping; a trade in every conceivable valuable high-
t carried on by a great multitude of traders; merchant
d harbour princes wielding as great financial power
erchants and princes of Europe. By conquering the
c points on the Asian sea routes, the Portuguese suc-
tablishing a colonial domain in that world, a weak em-
nevertheless was able to maintain itself with great vital-
entury. The Portuguese colonial regime, built by and
, coercion, and violence, did not at any point signify a
higher development' economically for Asian trade. The
al commercial structure continued to exist, however much
by religious wars breaking out between Moslems and
ns. Trade did not undergo any increase in quantity worthy
tion in the period. The commercial and economic forms of
rtuguese colonial regime were the same as those of Asian
and Asian authority: a trade relatively small in volume, con-
d by the government as a private enterprise, and all further
cise of authority existing only to insure the financial, fiscal ex-
tation of trade, shipping, and port traffic, with the higher of-
als and religious dignitaries recruited from the Portuguese aris-
cracy. Official exploitation, the economic policy of the colonial
gime, was feudal, then, not bourgeois commercial. The farming
f revenues on a large scale in practice transferred the exploitation
to the Indian and Persian Moslem wealthy merchants. The ordinary
Portuguese 'free burghers'—to use the Dutch [East India] Company term—carried on their handiwork, shipping, and craft trading side by side with and together with Asians. Ethnic intermixture
took place on a large scale.

The Portuguese colonial regime, then, did not introduce a single
new economic element into the commerce of southern Asia. The
forms of political and economic domination—monopolies, financial
exploitation, 'fiscalization' of the government—all of them originated in the caliphates and Byzantium, and were transferred to
Portugal, and perhaps carried on there, by Jews and Italians. The

political power of the Portuguese, based on their military supe[rior]ity, now made possible the large-scale application of those form[s in] Asia. That military superiority was the only thing the Portug[uese] carried overseas to Asia as a new and European element. Tho[ugh] the Portuguese period was the first of the European colonial peri[ods] which from then on were to decide the fate of Asia, this fact ser[ves] to separate it from the following, second period, that of Dutch a[nd] English overseas voyages and colonial settlement, and to link it [in] spirit and forms to the previous periods, those of purely Asi[an] trade. The Portuguese regime only introduced a non-intensi[ve] drain on the existing structure of shipping and trade. The ne[xt] period would in its time organize a new system of foreign trad[e] and foreign shipping, it would call into life trenchant colonial re[-] lationships, and it would create new economic forms in Europe— not perhaps as a direct result but rather as a parallel development bolstered by the system. Not Lisbon and Seville, but Amsterdam, Middleburg, Enkhuizen, and London were among the heralds of a new era.

4. The Spaniards in the Philippines

While the Portuguese were endeavoring to find a sea route to Asia by sailing southwards along the coast of Africa, the Spaniards, with the same objective, had been groping their way westwards across the Atlantic. It was however not until ten years after the Portuguese conquest of Malacca that Magellan, a Portuguese in the service of Spain, carried the Spanish flag westwards across the Pacific to the Philippines. When Spanish colonization of the islands commenced more than forty years later the greatest impact on Filipino society was made by the Christian missionaries. The following selection, reprinted by permission from John L. Phelan's book, The Hispanization of the Philippines (*University of Wisconsin Press, Madison, 1959, pp. 53-56 and 70-71*) *discusses certain aspects of the early imposition of Christianity on the Filipinos.*

Spanish missionaries viewed themselves as soldiers of Christ waging with spiritual weapons a war to overthrow the devil's tyranny over pagan peoples. They envisaged their work as a "spiritual conquest" of the minds and hearts of the natives, a supplement to, and the ultimate justification for, the military conquest. . . .

Christianity was presented to the infidels not as a more perfect expression of their pagan beliefs but as something entirely new. Any resemblance between the two religions was dismissed as a diabolical conspiracy in which the devil deceived unbelievers by mimicking the rituals and the beliefs of Christianity. The policy of breaking abruptly with the pagan past explains the vigor with which temples and idols were destroyed. The Spanish missionaries have been much criticized for this practice. Yet the religious were not modern archaeologists. In their eyes pagan artifacts were but the visible symbols of the devil's tyrannical dominion, and hence they merited destruction.

In the Philippines there were no temples to demolish. But sacred groves were cut down by zealous Spanish religious who were determined to break the magic sway such groves exercised over the Filipinos. And pagan idols by the thousands were committed to the flames by iconoclastic religious in the presence of bewildered and fascinated Filipinos. The dismantling of outward pagan observances was but the first step in the introduction of Christianity. . . .

The indigenous peoples with whom the Spaniards came in contact seldom showed any desire to abandon voluntarily their own religious values. Compulsion of some sort had to be employed. Given their Christian humanitarianism, the clergy usually protested against the use of force; but without coercion, or the threat of it, the natives in many cases would have rejected the appeals of the religious to discard paganism.

Sullen distrust but not armed defiance usually greeted the newly arrived missionary. . . .

Wherever the religious met morose distrust, they did not attempt to impose themselves on the elders of the community. What the religious usually requested was that some of the children be committed to their care. The chieftains might shun the monastery for some time, but out of a combination of curiosity and fear they would hand over some of their children to be educated by the religious. Evangelization followed a standard pattern. The children of the chieftains were first indoctrinated, and then the chieftains themselves were persuaded. With the conversion of the leaders of the community, the baptism of their followers came as a matter of course. . . .

The missionary enterprise got off to a very slow start between 1565 and 1578. During the first five years there were not more than one hundred baptisms. In 1576 there were only thirteen Augustinian friars, and their baptisms had been confined mostly to children. Linguistic ignorance, paucity of priests, and the missionary interest in China account for this lack of progress. The coming of the Franciscans in 1578 and the arrival of large contingents of Augustinians and Franciscans after 1578 produced a change in the scope and tempo of evangelical operations. The Franciscans were soon followed by the Dominicans and the Jesuits. The decisive decade was the one between 1576 and 1586. During this period the number of missionaries rose from 13 to 94, and by 1594 there were 267 regulars. The number of baptisms rose proportionately to the increase in missionary personnel, as the following approximate figures suggest:

1583	100,000	baptisms
1586	170,000	"
1594	286,000	"
1612	322,400	"
1622	500,000	"

Thus it took some fifty years of intensive missionary activity to lay the foundation of Philippine Christianity.

The Christianization of the Philippines falls into three periods. The years between 1565 and 1578 were preparatory and exploratory. There was a scarcity of missionary personnel, and those available were without adequate linguistic training. The decades from 1578 until 1609, after which date the Philippines began to feel the full impact of the Dutch war, were the "golden age" of the missionary enterprise. . . .

As the seventeenth century wore on, the inadequacies of the missionary effort became increasingly apparent. . . . Yet the Filipinos were Christianized in the face of the severe handicaps of a shortage of priests and a dispersed population speaking a bewildering variety of languages.

2

THE EXTENSION
OF WESTERN COLONIAL RULE
IN SOUTHEAST ASIA

The Dutch first entered the Southeast Asian trading preserves of the Iberian powers in mid-1596 when four ships under the command of Cornelis de Houtman anchored off Bantam in western Java. The action of the Spanish monarch Philip II in closing the Iberian ports to Dutch shipping after 1580 is the explanation usually advanced to account for Dutch participation in the direct trade with Asia, because it was from Lisbon that the Hollanders had been accustomed to collect cargoes of Indonesian spices for distribution throughout Europe. It seems more certain, however, that the exclusion of the Dutch from Lisbon and the disruption of Antwerp's commerce after 1569 provided only the occasion for the direct voyaging to Asia; the underlying cause is to be found in the rapid expansion of Dutch shipping and trade in Europe, especially with the Baltic, during the sixteenth century. This resulted in surpluses of capital, which found ready outlet in commercial ventures in Southeast Asia, when men like De Houtman and Jan Huyghen van Linschoten returned to Holland and placed their first-hand knowledge of Portuguese trade with Asia in the hands of the merchant capitalists of Amsterdam, Enkhuizen, Middleburg, Rotterdam, and Delft.

The first Dutch voyage to Southeast Asia was only marginally a financial success, but it demonstrated the fact that it was possible to collect spices and pepper direct from the sources of supply. During 1598 twenty-two ships left the Netherlands for the East, financed by local trading companies. Competition between these companies proved to be disadvantageous to trade and led to their incorporation in the United East India Company in 1602. The Company was established under monopoly charter of the States General, and, through its Seventeen Directors in the Netherlands and its agents abroad, it controlled Dutch colonial endeavors in Asia during the two ensuing centuries. Although initially cumbersome in its management and complex in its structure, the new Company soon developed into one of the most powerful trading organizations of the time. Compared to it, the English East India Company, founded in December, 1600, under royal charter for the same commercial objectives, was a small and limited venture.

5. British Trade in Indonesia During the Seventeenth Century

The first objective of the officials of the Dutch East India Company was to drive their Portuguese and British rivals out of Southeast Asia. They managed to negotiate treaties with some of the Indonesian rulers of the Spice Islands, and in 1623 succeeded temporarily in removing the representatives of the British Company from the Moluccas. Contrary to the statements made in most of the standard histories, the "Massacre of Amboina" did not have the effect of totally eliminating British traders from eastern Indonesia, as the following selection, reprinted by permission from "The 'Amboyna Massacre' of 1623" by Dr. D. K. Bassett in Journal of Southeast Asian History *(I, 2, 1960, pp. 8-9) shows. The Spaniards who retained a base in the Moluccas until the 1660s also continued to do business in spices.*

One of the reasons why so much significance has been attached to the Amboyna "Massacre" as the termination of English commercial ambitions in South East Asia has been a general ignorance of subsequent events; little has been known of the details of English activity in the East Indies after 1623, possibly because the superior attraction of the Indian mainland has proved as irresistible to the historian as it did to the Company itself. To assume, however, that because nothing of importance is known to have occurred in the East Indies in the later seventeenth century, nothing of importance can have taken place, is surely dangerous and fallacious reasoning. The neglect of the post-1623 period can also be explained on the basis of a premise which deserves more sympathy but had equally little foundation. This is the belief that profitable trade in the East Indies was synonymous with the trade in spices, i.e. cloves, mace and nutmeg; once the islands producing those commodities passed under Dutch political control, little else of commercial importance remained. Such an attitude would, of course, imply that pepper, which grew extensively in Java, Borneo and Sumatra, was a trivial investment, but it has been pointed out that as late as 1650 pepper constituted over fifty [per cent] of the value of Dutch cargoes from Batavia to Europe. Hence, even assuming that the Dutch monopoly of spices after 1623 was sufficiently effective to compel the English Company to place the bulk of its investment in pepper, this would still not mean that the English East Indies' trade was financially unimportant. If one could go further and prove that the closing of the English factories in the Spice Islands did not in fact involve the exclusion of the English Company from the spice trade for another twenty years, the traditional interpretation of the Amboyna "Massacre" would be largely untenable.

It has always been taken for granted that the volume of English trade with Indonesia after 1623 must have been negligible compared to the volume of the trade before the Amboyna tragedy. Nothing could be more erroneous. The number of English ships which left Java with cargoes for London in the fifteen trading seasons from 1602 to 1616 was 28, of which one ship was lost without trace and another was wrecked upon the coast of Brittany; these ships represented a combined tonnage of a little over 10,000 tons, of which about 660 tons was lost at sea. The comparative number of ships dispatched from Bantam to London during the nineteen possible trading seasons from 1659 to 1681 (1665-1667 and 1673 were war years when shipping was not sent out from England) was 87, of which four were lost. This second group of ships represented an aggregate of about 34,000 tons, of which some 1,500 tons was lost at sea. Even when allowance is made for the slight difference in the number of trading seasons, it will be seen that the number of English ships engaged in the trade between Indonesia and England was two and a half times greater in the later period than in 1602-1616, while the tonnage had increased almost three fold. Even during the less vigorous decades of the 1630's and 1640's an average of two or three ships left Bantam for London every year, while in times of unusual activity, as in 1648-1650, 14 ships were sent home in three seasons. It is true that the Company's trade in Indonesia was virtually at a standstill between 1652-1658, but this was the result of abnormal conditions caused by the first Anglo-Dutch war (1652-1654), the Dutch blockade of Bantam (1656-1659), and the disturbed political atmosphere of England under Cromwell. After the East India Company's charter was renewed by Cromwell in 1657 and again by the restored Charles II in 1661, the directors were quick to expand the volume of their trade with Indonesia to the highest level it ever reached in the seventeenth century.

6. The British Colonial System in West Sumatra

This situation did not obtain long. In 1682, following a dynastic dispute in the Bantam sultanate, in which the British and the Dutch took different sides, the Dutch were able at long last to exclude their British rivals from west Java altogether. It took the British three years to find another trading base in Indonesia, this time at Benkulen on Sumatra's west coast. Here, during the late seventeenth, eighteenth, and early nineteenth centuries, they were able to extend their territorial possessions along three hundred miles of the coast and establish a colonial system based on the forced cultivation of pepper. The next selection is taken from William Marsden's The History of Sumatra (London, 1811, 3rd edition, pp. 129-130 and 139-141). This book, one of the classics of Southeast Asian historiography, was first published in 1783 when Marsden was twenty-nine years of age. He writes with first-hand experience of the forced system of pepper cultivation in west Sumatra for he served in the East India Company's secretariat at Benkulen between 1771 and 1779.

Of those productions of Sumatra, which are regarded as articles of commerce, the most important and most abundant is pepper. This is the object of the East India Company's trade thither, and this alone it keeps in its own hands; its servants, and merchants under its protection, being free to deal in every other commodity.

Many of the princes or chiefs in different parts of the island having invited the English to form settlements in their respective districts, [trading] factories were accordingly established, and a permanency and regularity thereby given to the trade, which was very uncertain whilst it depended upon the success of occasional voyages to the coast; disappointments ensuing not only from failure of adequate quantities of pepper to furnish cargoes when required, but also from the caprices and chicanery of the chiefs with whom the disposal of it lay, the motives of whose conduct could not be understood by those who were unacquainted with the language and manners of the people. These inconveniencies were obviated when the agents of the Company were enabled, by their residence on the spot, to obtain an influence in the country, to inspect the state of the plantations, secure the collection of the produce, and make an estimate of the tonnage necessary for its conveyance to Europe.

In order to bind the chiefs to the observance of their original promises and professions, and to establish a plausible and legal claim, in opposition to the attempts of rival European powers to interfere in the trade of the same country, written contracts, attended with much form and solemnity, were entered into with the former; by which they engaged to oblige all their dependants to cultivate pepper, and to secure to us the exclusive purchase of it; in return for which they were to be protected from their enemies, supported in the rights of sovereignty, and to be paid a certain allowance or custom, on the produce of their respective territories.

The price for many years paid to the cultivators for their produce, was ten Spanish dollars or fifty shillings per *bahar* of five hundred weight or five hundred and sixty pounds. About the year 1780, with a view to their encouragement and the increase of investment, as it is termed, the sum was augmented to fifteen dollars. To this cost is to be added the custom above-mentioned, varying in different districts according to specific agreements, but amounting in general to one dollar and an half, or two dollars on each *bahar,* which is distributed amongst the chiefs at an annual entertainment; and presents are made at the same time to planters who have distinguished themselves by their industry. This low price, at which the natives submit to cultivate the plantations, affording to each man an income of not more than from eight to twelve dollars yearly, and the undisturbed monopoly we have so long possessed of the trade, from near *Indrapura* northward to Flat Point southward [near Belimbing at the southern tip of the island], are doubtless in a principal degree to be attributed to the peculiar manner in which this part of the island is shut up, by the surfs which prevail along the south-west coast, from communication with strangers, whose competition would naturally produce the effect of enhancing the price of the commodity. . . .

Once in every year, a survey of all the pepper-plantations is taken by the Company's European servants, resident at the various settlements, in the neighbourhood of which that article is cultivated. The number of vines in each particular garden is counted; accurate observation is made of its state and condition; orders are given, where necessary, for further care, for completion of stipulated quantity, renewals, changes of situation for better soil; and rewards and punishments are distributed to the planters, as they appear, from the degree of their industry or remissness, deserving of either. Minutes of all these are entered in the survey-book, which, beside giving present information to the chief, and to the [British] governor and council [at Benkulen], to whom a copy is transmitted, serves as a guide and check for the survey of the succeeding year. An abstract of the form of the book is as follows. It is divided into sundry columns, containing the name of the village; the names of the planters; the number of chinkareens[1] planted; the number of vines just planted; of young vines, not in a bearing state, three classes or years; of young vines in a bearing state, three classes; of vines in prime; of those on decline; of those that are old, but still productive; the total number; and lastly the quantity of pepper received during the year. A space is left for occasional remarks, and at the conclusion is subjoined a comparison of the totals of each column, for the whole district or residency, with those of the pre-

_____
[1] Vegetating props for the pepper vines. [ED.]

ceding year. This business the reader will perceive to be attended with considerable trouble, exclusive of the actual fatigue of the surveys, which, from the nature of the country, must necessarily be performed on foot, in a climate not very favourable to such excursions. The journeys in few places can be performed in less than a month, and often require a much longer time.

The arrival of the Company's Resident at each *dusun*[2] is considered as a period of festivity. The chief, together with the principal inhabitants, entertain him and his attendants with rustic hospitality, and when he retires to rest, his slumbers are soothed, or interrupted, by the songs of young females, who never fail to pay this compliment to the respected guest; and receive in return some trifling ornamental and useful presents (such as looking-glasses, fans, and needles) at his departure.

The inhabitants, by the original contracts of the head men with the Company, are obliged to plant a certain number of vines; each family one thousand, and each young unmarried man five hundred; and, in order to keep up the succession of produce, so soon as their gardens attain to their prime state, they are ordered to prepare others, that they may begin to bear as the old ones fall off; but as this can seldom be enforced, till the decline becomes evident, and as young gardens are liable to various accidents which older ones are exempt from, the succession is rendered incomplete, and the consequence is, that the annual produce of each district fluctuates, and is greater or less, in the proportion of the quantity of bearing vines to the whole number.

7. Dutch Policy Toward the Indonesian Rulers

As will be readily understood, the British exerted considerable influence on the economic life of the peoples of west Sumatra during the seventeenth and eighteenth centuries. The Dutch, too, were rapidly extending their economic and political frontiers in Indonesia during these years as they came to assume increasing territorial commitments. Unlike the Portuguese and Spaniards, the Dutch were not interested in the task of Christian conversion; all

---

[2] Village. [ED.]

they wanted was a quick turnover of their investment. They under-stood that the acquisition of territory adversely affected profits be-cause of the increased cost of administration; they found, however, that, in order to establish stable conditions in which to conduct their commercial operations, they were obliged to interfere in the affairs of the Southeast Asian rulers.

The nature of the control exercised by the Dutch in Indonesia was largely determined by the mercantile character of the East India Company itself. Originally the Dutch paid money for tropical produce such as pepper, spices, coffee, and rice which was needed by the Company for its trading transactions. Realizing, however, that the direct collection of this produce and the close supervision and administration of the Indonesian people involved heavy fi-nancial burdens for the Company, the Dutch generally left the in-digenous rulers in effective control of their districts. These rulers, who were called regents by the Dutch after their own officials in the Netherlands, were under treaty obligations to their Western masters to see that the Indonesian peasantry obeyed their orders for planting the export crops and delivering the requisite amounts of produce annually. Otherwise, they were left fairly free in the ad-ministration of their districts, except in the Priangan regions of west Java where various attempts were made by the Dutch during the eighteenth century to effect closer supervision of the coffee cul-tivation by the appointment of Supervisors and Coffee Sergeants. It was the task of these men to see that the various regulations of the Company were enforced, but they were so poorly paid that what generally happened was that they formed alliances with the In-donesian regents and concocted accounts to their own advantage. The following selection, which describes eighteenth-century Dutch policy toward the Indonesian rulers, is reprinted by permission from B. Schrieke's Indonesian Sociological Studies *(W. van Hoeve, Ltd., The Hague, 1955, I, pp. 202-206). Schrieke's account provides one of the best insights into the colonial policy of the Netherlands during this early phase of Western rule in Southeast Asia.*

Up to the time of [H. W.] Daendels' governor-generalship (1808-1811), a difference existed between the regents of the northeast coast of Java and those in Priangan as regards their relationship to the Company. The former signed a deed of alliance, referred to by Daendels as a 'contract'—which, however, merely contained a summary of obligations—, and had to meet the so-called quotas. The regents of Priangan received a certificate of appointment and had to see to deliveries. Daendels put an end to this distinction. However, he maintained the so-called 'Priangan system', which the Company had inaugurated, as did also the English interim government [in 1811-16 under T. S. Raffles].[1] Even after the introduction of land rent in other areas, the system remained unaltered in principle, until 1871. (Van den Bosch's culture system of 1830 was inspired by it.)[2] In the main the Priangan system amounted to the following: the government levied no taxation in Priangan, but the population there was obliged to cultivate and deliver supplies of coffee to the government at a price the government itself fixed; the native regents received no salary but were authorized to raise taxes from the population on condition that they paid the salaries of the subordinate native heads.

In the days of the [Dutch East India] Company, the disparity between the legal position of the regents of the northeast coast of Java and of those of Priangan, to which disparity Daendels put an end, did not however make any practical difference in the government's attitude towards the regents nor in the way in which they were treated by government officials. . . .

Initially, trade remained the prime object—the Company wanted products. If the delivery of the products was irregular, the procedure was to 'exhort' the regents to deliver. It was not long, however, before stronger language was being used. . . .

Whereas the prices paid for products were originally fixed by negotiation with the regents, these were soon being determined by the government alone and forced on the regents as a unilateral regulation. The government decided what and how much had to be delivered and the regents had to see that everything was done as required.

The compulsory cultures which resulted from this procedure soon called for inspection and improvement and were therefore subjected to supervision. Tours of inspection were made for the pur-

[1] See Selection 9.
[2] See Selections 10 and 11.

pose. The Company took upon itself more and more the allure of a sovereign power. At periodic intervals the regents were obliged to come and pay their respects at Batavia. Moreover, disputes between the regents themselves induced the Company to intervene and settle matters. It hesitated all the same to punish regents for neglect of their duties. For whereas economic motives forced the Company to interfere within the province of the regents' authority, political considerations caused it to abstain. The more the Company's authority established itself (1705), however, the more economic interests secured the upper hand. For that matter, the Company's local officials already allowed themselves to go further in dealing with the native heads than the government in Batavia dared. From December, 1704 onwards the Priangan regents received certificates of appointment, but their instructions remained vague. In those days the regents were in practice only dimly aware of their subordination to a sovereign, supervising power. Gradually, however, their powers were curtailed. They were no longer permitted to appoint the district chiefs themselves, even though they had to provide their salaries. [Governor-General G. W.] Van Imhoff [1743 to 1750] concerned himself with the internal administration of the regencies. First the [Dutch] resident of Cheribon and later the government interfered energetically even with the reserved right of the regents to administer justice, so that nothing remained, for instance, of their judicial powers in penal affairs. They were treated more and more as officials. With the requisitioning of compulsory deliveries of coffee at a greatly reduced price determined by the Company, the government's voice had, indeed, already become more commanding. In 1726 the native heads were forbidden "most strictly, on pain of being put in chains" to uproot coffee bushes "since they were rooted on Company land which they have in their possession only by virtue of the Company's goodwill until further notice, and whose usufruct they enjoy." The decline in cultivation, which resulted from the reduction in price, was attributed to the extortions of the native rulers. The appointment of European overseers was therefore considered. When, a few years later, a surplus was feared, the native rulers were then compelled to destroy the coffee bushes and to switch over to the cultivation of pepper instead. In 1789 they were issued with instructions for cultivation and overseers carried out inspections to see that those instructions were adhered to, their income being made partly dependent upon the output of coffee. In the meantime the regents were falling ever more deeply into the Company's debt, in part because of the system of advances. In 1800 they were informed of "the government's legitimate displeasure" at the small coffee crop, which was attributed to carelessness in plucking, collection, and delivery. The regent of Chianjur was threatened with the government's wrath if he failed to do his best "to make good the past by energetic action." The regents were made responsible and threatened with punishment in the event of failure. Regents were now on repeated occasions even dismissed. Supervision and inspection were intensified. Action had to be taken against extortionist practices on the part of the regents. With the introduction of annual inspections the expressions of dissatisfaction and serious reprimands became more frequent. The Priangan regents were entirely dependent upon the commissioner of native affairs. . . .

They were often obliged to suffer the grossest discourtesies. Moreover, fines were imposed upon them "for their omissions" (which fines found their way into the commissioner's pocket) in order "to keep them under a bond of obedience which was reasonable and absolutely essential." . . .

The number of European overseers (usually ex-soldiers with the rank of sergeant) was increased and their income made entirely dependent upon the production of coffee in their area. It goes without saying that these men, too, often interfered quite freely in the affairs of the regents, even though they were officially their subordinates. The instruction of 1789, meanwhile, went as far as to make the overseers responsible for the general supervision of the regents' official conduct. Arbitrary action on their part against lower native officials, without consultation of the regents themselves, was far from uncommon.

The government was not much given to theorizing about the actual nature of its position. It wanted, as far as possible, to remain simply a merchant and to involve itself as little as it could with administrative affairs. It preferred to regard even the compulsory cultivation and delivery of coffee in Priangan as a commercial transaction.

8. The Spanish Colonial System
in the Philippines

The commercial objectives which colored Dutch colonial policy and practice in Indonesia during the eighteenth century should not be measured by an emotional yardstick. There were, after all, certain economic advantages gained by the Indonesian peoples themselves. In western Java, for example, the Dutch paid to the cultivators there and in southern Sumatra something like 12½ million Spanish dollars for the 316 million pounds of pepper they collected during the late seventeenth and eighteenth centuries. It is true that a large proportion of this money went into the pockets of the Indonesian rulers, but the Dutch themselves paid for the produce at something approaching market rates. Nor were the Dutch the only Westerners in Southeast Asia who used forced cultivation methods which, by and large, represented an extension of the existing indigenous systems; as we have seen, the British themselves operated a colonial system in western Sumatra during the seventeenth, eighteenth, and early nineteenth centuries which was based on similar principles to those employed by the Dutch.

In the Philippines essentially different colonial principles were adopted. Following their conquest of, and settlement on, Cebu in 1565, the Spaniards gradually extended their territorial control in the Philippines. In 1569 Masbate, Ticao, and Burias were subdued, and in the following year expeditions were mounted against Mindoro and the important town of Manila. It was not until mid-1571, however, that Manila was finally captured, and the work of pacification of the whole island of Luzon commenced. The following selection, taken from Gregorio F. Zaide's book, Philippine Political and Cultural History *(Philippine Education Company, Manila, 1957, I, pp. 158, 160-165, 168-174, and 179-180), presents an over-all political and economic assessment of Spanish colonization as seen through the eyes of a Filipino historian. The selection is reprinted by permission.*

The first and most outstanding aim of Spanish colonization was to spread Christianity. . . . Economic wealth and political grandeur, although coveted by the Spanish kings and conquistadores, were to Spain secondary colonial aims.

[Another] aim of Spanish colonization was the aspiration for political grandeur. By acquiring the Philippines, Spain emerged as a mighty empire whose frontiers straddled both hemispheres, and Philip II (1556-98) thus became the first European monarch who could justly boast that the sun never set on his dominions. . . .

For over 300 years the Philippines was a crown colony of Spain. Until 1821, when the Mexicans revolted and won their independence from Spain, she was in a sense a dependency of Mexico, being administered by the Mexican viceroy in the name of the Spanish king. From 1821 to 1898, she was a distinct governmental unit under the direct control of the home government at Madrid. The king as sovereign issued *cedulas* (decrees) for the administration of the colony and appointed the governor, the members of the Royal Audiencia, and other high colonial officials.

In Spain, Philippine affairs were in charge of the *Consejo de Indias* (Council of the Indies) which, in conjunction with the king, legislated for all Spanish colonies. This council also served as the high court of appeal to which all cases of importance from the colonies came for final adjudication. It was established in 1524 and abolished in 1826. After various changes, the Philippines was placed under the *Ministerio de Ultramar* (Ministry of the Colonies) in 1863. Its head, called *Ministro de Ultramar* (Minister of the Colonies), was assisted by the *Consejo de Filipinas* (Council of the Philippines) sitting in Madrid. This Council, which drafted decrees and suggested reforms, was composed of the sub-secretary and directors of the Ministry of the Colonies as members *ex-officio* and 12 other members selected by the king because of their knowledge of colonial matters. . . .

Except for brief periods (1810-13, 1820-23, 1834-37), the Philippines did not enjoy the benefits of the Spanish Constitution and the privilege of representation in the Spanish *Cortes* (parliament). In other words, the colony was governed by special laws which consisted of the king's royal decrees, the governor's executive proclamations, and the laws of Spain extended to the Philippines by royal sanction. . . .

At the head of the centralized government established by Spain in the Philippines was the Governor and Captain-General, who symbolized the might and [majesty] of the Spanish Crown. He was appointed, and removed from office, by the king. At first he received an annual salary of 8,000 pesos, which subsequently was increased to 40,000 pesos with liberal allowances. He exercised great powers—executive, military, judicial, and religious. In his capacity as governor, he had the right to control and supervise all administrative offices, and to appoint colonial officials not named by the king. As captain-general, he was commander-in-chief of all armed forces, with the special duty of providing for the national defense of the Philippines. As president of the Royal Audiencia of Manila until 1861 he had a hand in the dispensation of justice. He was the royal vice-patron, and, as such, he assumed the king's ecclesiastical authority over church offices and missions. His other powers included the collection and administration of public revenues, the promulgation of regulations for the observance of local officials, the pardoning of criminal offenders, and the supervision of trade and industries. One great power of the governor was the *cumplase* by which he could suspend or disregard any royal decree or law from Spain. . . .

In administering the Philippines, the governor was assisted by two advisory bodies—the Board of Authorities (*Junta de Autoridades*) and the Council for Administration (*Consejo de Administración*). The former, which was the cabinet, was established by the royal decree of April 16, 1850. It was composed of the governor-general as president, the archbishop of Manila, the general second in command, the admiral of the navy, the intendant of the treasury, the director-general of the civil administration, the president of the *Audiencia*, and the attorney-general. Its chief function was to advise the governor-general on questions of unusual importance.

The Council of Administration, a consultative body of larger representation, was created by the royal order of July 4, 1861. It was composed of the governor-general as president; the archbishop of Manila; the general second in command; the admiral of the navy; the president of the *Audiencia;* the intendant of the treasury; the director-general of the civil administration; the fathers superior of the religious orders; the president of the Manila chamber of commerce; the president of the Economic Society of Friends of the

Country; three delegated members from Luzon; three delegated members from the Visayas; and four other members appointed by the Crown. Its functions were to deliberate on the government budgets, the questions of royal patronage, and other matters which the governor might deem proper to submit to it for opinion. . . .

At the inception of her rule, Spain transplanted to the Philippines the medievalistic economic organization known as the *encomienda,* which strikingly resembled Europe's feudal system, with the *encomienda* itself simulating the fief; the *encomendero,* the feudal lord; and the Filipinos, the vassals. The *encomienda* was a piece of territory, including its inhabitants and resources, which the Spanish king granted to the *conquistadores* and colonizers as a reward for their services to the Crown. The holder of the *encomienda* was known as *encomendero.* . . .

The *encomiendas* were of two kinds: *royal,* belonging to the king, and *private,* owned by private persons. . . .

The first *encomiendas* were assigned by [Miguel Lopez de] Legazpi in Cebu in 1571 when, acting upon royal order, he apportioned certain regions of that island to his soldiers. As rapidly as the Philippines was pacified, more and more *encomiendas* were given to the Spaniards. . . . In 1591 there were in the Philippines 257 *encomiendas* (31 royal and 236 private) containing 667,612 inhabitants and 166,903 tributes. In 1621 the number of *encomiendas* decreased to 186 on account of the death of their holders and their transformation into provinces; in these *encomiendas* there were 523,572 inhabitants and 130,938 tributes. . . .

The Spanish *encomenderos,* like the feudal barons, ruled their *encomiendas* as if they were petty monarchs. They collected the tributes, supervised labor in the public works, and maintained peace and order. According to the laws of the Indies, they were obligated to protect and educate the Filipinos under their charge, to safeguard the latter's welfare and happiness, and to aid the missionaries in the propagation of Christianity. It came to pass, however, that the *encomenderos* became abusive and rapacious. The poor Filipinos under them were cheated, flogged, maltreated, neglected, overtaxed, and overworked. Not only did they force these helpless people to pay excessive tribute and render burdensome labor, but also they committed tyrannical acts on them and failed to aid the missionaries in converting and educating them. Instead of being the guardians and protectors of the Filipinos, the *encomenderos* became their exploiters. . . .

From the days of Legazpi to 1884, the Filipinos paid the tribute (*tributo*), a kind of head-tax, to Spain. The rate was originally eight *reales* per family payable in money or in kind; it was raised to ten *reales* in 1602, and to twelve *reales* in 1851. One tribute was equivalent to one family consisting of the husband, wife, and minor children. Every married man over 20 years old (in 1851 reduced to 18 years) or every unmarried woman over 25 years of age (in 1851 reduced to 20 years) living with the parents was considered "half-tribute." All Spanish residents, Filipino officials (notably *cabezas de barangay*), soldiers and seamen, widows of Spaniards, descendants of Lakan-Dula and other loyal Filipino rulers in the past, priests and nuns, and paupers were exempted from paying the tribute.

In addition to the regular tribute, the Filipinos paid one *real* for tithes (*diezmos prediales*), originally corresponding to $\frac{1}{10}$ of the fruits or income of the land; one *real* for the community funds (*caja de comunidad*); and three *reales* for the church (*sanctorum*). From 1655 to 1850 they also paid a special war tax of one-half *real* called *Donativo de Zamboanga;* this tax was used exclusively to finance the campaigns against the Moros.

The Filipinos hated the tribute and often rose in rebellion against it. The rate of the tribute was reasonable; insofar as this rate was concerned, they were willing and able to pay it. What made the tribute odious to them was the humiliating purpose for which it was levied, that is, recognition of their vassalage to Spain. Another objection to the tribute was the unjust manner employed in its collection. The *encomenderos,* who collected it, made great profit for themselves by forcing the people to pay in rice, clothes, fowls, or other produce and later reselling these commodities at exorbitant prices. In many cases also the tribute collectors cheated the people as to the amount of the tribute, as illustrated by the case of an *encomendero* of Dagami in Leyte who compelled the Filipinos to pay the annual tribute in wax and used a tampered balance in weighing it so that the people actually paid double the amount of atrocities, such as torturing and even killing the people, plundering the tribute. In collecting the tribute, the *encomenderos* committed

their homes and fields, and confiscating their carabaos and other property. . . .

Besides paying the tribute, the Filipinos rendered forced labor as another manifestation of their vassalage to Spain. This labor, known as *polo,* was said to have originated in 1496 when Columbus forced the natives of Hispaniola who could not pay him gold as tribute to work in the Spanish settlements. As the system operated in the Philippines, all Filipinos from 16 to 60 years of age, excluding the females, rendered forced labor for 40 days a year, such as building and repairing roads, bridges, churches, and other public works; cutting timber in the forests; and working in artillery foundries and shipyards. Any *polista* (one who rendered obligatory labor) could be exempted only upon payment of one *real* and a half per day during the 40 days he was supposed to be at work; this sum of money paid in lieu of actual labor was called *falla.*

The Spanish king regulated the forced labor by just laws, but said [laws] were generally ignored by the colonial officials. Like the collection of tribute, the *polo* system became a source of Spanish abuses and corruption. The Filipinos, while at work, were supposed to be paid one-fourth *real* a day and supplied with free rice. Usually, however, the officials grabbed both money and rice ration for themselves. Oftentimes, they snatched the Filipinos from their homes and fields and compelled them to work in far-away shipyards and to serve as rowers and fighters in Spanish expeditions to foreign lands. Many of these Filipinos never saw their beloved families again because they had died in distant shores fighting for the glory of Spain, and those who [were] fortunate to return home safely were impressed again for other services. . . .

One of the best achievements of Spain in the Philippines during the early years of her colonization was the abolition of slavery. The laws of the Indies, especially those promulgated in 1526, 1541, and 1588, prohibited and penalized slavery in all Spanish colonies. However, these laws were not effectively carried out so that Philip II issued a royal decree dated August 9, 1589 ordering the emancipation of all slaves in the Philippines. This decree was strengthened by a bull of Pope Gregory XIV, issued at Rome on April 18, 1591, which threatened to excommunicate those persons who would not liberate their slaves. . . .

Many authors of contemporary times, writing with superficial knowledge and biased perspective, have bitterly censured and uncharitably condemned the 300-year colonial record of Spain in the Philippines. It is true that the Spanish colonial system had certain defects, notably the absence of the spirit of progress, the prevalence of abuses and corruption in the civil service, the maladministration of justice, the absence of intellectual freedom, the failure to develop the natural resources, and the undemocratic denial of social and political rights to Filipinos. But these defects, it should be borne in mind, were really defects of the times. "Spanish failure, if such there be[,]" declared Justice [George A.] Malcolm, American jurist and historian, "at least merits a decent trial and a just verdict. Indeed the ideals existent during the height of Spanish power are so contrary to those of the present age that a fair comparison is impossible. One must in all justice remember that Spain could give no more than she herself possessed. In a state of decline herself, Spain could not govern the Philippines any more wisely, until she had cut out the decay of the home government."

The Spanish colonization in the Philippines, if judged in the light of the times in which it flourished and by taking into consideration its counter-balancing merits, can stand comparison with the colonial work of England, France, and Holland. While the English and Dutch colonizers were concerned only with the exploitation of the human and natural resources in Malaysia and India, Spain stressed the spiritual salvation and cultural uplift of the Filipinos. It is to the lasting glory of Spain that the annals of her Philippine colonization are not marred by the horrors of exploitation and slavery that blacken the colonial record of the European powers in the Far East, Africa, and the West Indies. She did not brutalize the Filipinos. Although she imposed her rule over them, she took great care to respect their customs and institutions. For all the blunders committed by her colonizers, she more than made up by imparting to the people the lasting legacies of the Christian religion and European civilization.

3

COLONIAL CONSOLIDATION
AND EXPLOITATION

On December 31, 1799, the most powerful of the early engines of Western imperialism, the Dutch East India Company, was formally dissolved. During the two centuries of its existence its economic foundations had never been subjected to official scrutiny so that its soundness as a commercial organization tended to be gauged by the dividends declared annually by the Seventeen Directors. This proved to be a dangerous criterion because dividends were kept at an artificially high level through the manipulation of loans, so as to obscure the Company's increasing indebtedness. During the middle years of the eighteenth century these debts amounted to more than ten million guilders; forty years later, when the Batavian Republic took over the control of the Company's affairs, this figure had increased tenfold. The debts had been incurred partly as a result of the developing burdens of administration during the second half of the eighteenth century, particularly after the disintegration and division of the old Javanese empire of Mataram in the middle of the century, partly because of the inefficient organization of the Company itself, partly because of the general decline in Dutch maritime resources, and partly as a result of increasing British competition in the trade of Southeast Asia.

The Fourth Anglo-Dutch War (1780-84) and the British naval blockade isolated Java from its European markets with devastating consequences to the Dutch East India Company. During the following decade, the French invaded the Netherlands and, until the end of the Napoleonic Wars, Holland existed as a mere appendage of France. Its colonial possessions in Southeast Asia were subsequently viewed by Great Britain as potential seats of hostile power, so that the Dutch settlements of Malacca (captured from the Portuguese in 1641) and Padang (on Sumatra's west coast) were seized in 1795, and in the following year the Moluccas were taken from the Dutch with the object of destroying their monopoly of fine spices once and for all. British power in Southeast Asia was extended even further in 1811 when Java and its dependencies were occupied, and an interim administration was established under a vigorous young governor, Thomas Stamford Raffles.

9. *The British Colonial System in Java,*
1811 to 1816

During the five years that the British remained in Java, a sweeping reform of the old Dutch colonial system was attempted. In his two-volume work, The History of Java (*London, 1817, I, pp. 152-159*), *Raffles outlined the course of these reforms, which had as their object the introduction into Java of a land rent system based upon free labor and free cultivation in place of the Dutch system of demanding tropical produce through forced deliveries and contingents.*

When the British arms prevailed in 1811, the attention of government was immediately turned to the state and the interests of its new subjects. It saw at once the natural advantages of the island and the causes which obstructed its prosperity, and it determined to effect those changes which, having succeeded in Western India, and being sanctioned by justice and expediency, were likely to improve those advantages and to remove those obstructions. . . .

The peasant was subject to gross oppression and undefined exaction: our object was to remove his oppressor, and to limit demand to a fixed and reasonable rate of contribution. He was liable to restraints on the freedom of inland trade, to personal services and forced contingents: our object was to commute them all for a fixed and well-known contribution. The exertions of his industry were reluctant and languid, because he had little or no interest in its fruits: our object was to encourage that industry, by connecting its exertions with the promotion of his own individual welfare and prosperity. Capital could not be immediately created, nor agricultural skill acquired; but by giving the cultivator a security, that whatever he accumulated would be for his own benefit, and whatever improvement he made, he or his family might enjoy it, a motive was held out to him to exert himself in the road to attain both. Leases, or contracts for fixed rents for terms of years, in the commencement, and eventually in perpetuity, seemed to be the only mode of satisfying the cultivator, that he would not be liable, as formerly, to yearly undefined demands; while freedom from all taxes but an assessment on his crop, or rather a fixed sum in commutation thereof, would leave him at full liberty to devote the whole of his attention and labour to render his land as productive as possible.

In conformity with these views, an entire revolution was effected in the mode of levying the revenue, and assessing the taxes upon agriculture. The foundation of the amended system was, 1st. The entire abolition of forced deliveries at inadequate rates, and of all feudal services, with the establishment of a perfect freedom in cultivation and trade: 2nd. The assumption, on the part of government, of the immediate superintendance of the lands, with the collection of the resources and rents thereof: 3rd. The renting out of the lands so assumed to the actual occupants, in large or small estates according to local circumstances, on leases for a moderate term. In the course of the following years (1814 and 1815) these measures were carried into execution in most of the districts under our government, with a view to the eventual establishment of a perpetual settlement, on the principle of the *ryotwar*,[1] or as it has been termed on Java, the *tiáng-álit* system.

The principles of land rental and detailed settlement were few and simple. After mature inquiry, no obstacle appeared to exist,

---

[1] The so-called *Ryotwari* system of land rent collection was developed in the Madras provinces of India by the British at the end of the eighteenth and beginning of the nineteenth centuries. The main principles of the system involved the assessment of individual land leases and the collection of land rents direct from the peasants, or *ryots*, without any intermediate agency. [ED.]

either in law or usage, to the interference of government, in regulating the condition of the peasantry; and it was resolved, therefore, that it should take into its own hands the management of that share of the land produce which was allowed to be its due, and protect the cultivator in the enjoyment and free disposal of the remainder. The undue power of the chiefs was to be removed, and so far as they had a claim for support, founded either on former services or deprivation of expected employment, they were to be remunerated in another way. The lands, after being surveyed and estimated, were to be parcelled out among the inhabitants of the villages, in the proportions established by custom or recommended by expediency. Contracts were to be entered into with each individual cultivator, who was to become the tenant of government, and leases specifying the extent and situation of their land, with the conditions of their tenure, were to be granted for one or more years, with a view to permanency, if at the end of the stipulated term, the arrangement should be found to combine the interest of the public revenue with the welfare and increasing prosperity of the occupant. If that was not the case, room was thus left for a new adjustment, for a reduction of rate, or for any change in the system which might adapt it more to the interests and wishes of the people, without prejudice to the rights of government.

The experiment hazarded nothing, and held out every prospect of success; it committed no injustice, and compromized no claim. The peasantry could not suffer, because an assessment less in amount, and levied in a less oppressive manner than formerly (all rents, taxes, and services included), was required of them: the chiefs could not complain, because they were allowed the fair emoluments of office, and only restrained from oppressions which did not so much benefit themselves as injure their inferiors. Most of the latter were not only allowed an equivalent for their former income, but employed in services allied to their former duties,—the collection of the revenue, and the superintendance of the police. As the cultivator had acquired rights which the chief could not violate, as the former held in his possession a lease with the conditions on which he cultivated his farm, no infringement of which could be attempted on the part of the latter with impunity, no evil could result from employing the chiefs in collecting the revenue of dis-

tricts, while, from their practical knowledge of the habits and individual concerns of the peasantry, of the nature of the seasons and
the crops, they were the fittest persons for the office. For these
services it seemed most expedient to pay them, either by allowing
them a certain per-centage on their collections, or by allotting them
portions of land rent free. The village constitution (which will be
more particularly noticed in treating of the institutions of the
country) was preserved inviolate; and the chiefs or head men of the
villages, in many instances elected by the free will of the villagers,
were invariably continued in office as the immediate collectors of
the rents, and with sufficient authority to preserve the police, and
adjust the petty disputes that might arise within them; the government scrupulously avoiding all unnecessary interference in the
customs, usages, and details of these societies. . . . In the first
settlement, leases were only granted for a year, or at the utmost
three years, and were given to intermediate renters; but in the
more detailed settlement of 1814, after sufficient information had
been collected on the state of the country, government determined
to act directly with the individual cultivator, and to lay the foundation of a permanent system. By this latter period, the experiments
had been tried to a certain extent, and had succeeded beyond the
most sanguine expectation. Difficulties met us in the way, but they
were by no means insurmountable: there were at first imperfec-
tions in the system, but they did not affect its principle and were
easily removed. By the zeal, the ability, and industry of the various
officers entrusted with the execution of the duty, whatever was
practicable in furtherance of the object in which they felt deeply
interested, was accomplished. In the course of the years 1814 and
1815, the new system was introduced into *Bantam, Chéribon,* and the
eastern districts, over a population of a million and a half of cultivators, not only without disturbance and opposition, but to the
satisfaction of all classes of the natives, and to the manifest increase
of the public revenue derivable from land. In several journies
which I undertook into the different provinces, for the purposes of
examining in person the effect of the progressive system of reform
which I had the happiness to introduce, and of lending the sanction of official authority to such modifications of it as local circumstances might render advisable, I was a pleased spectator of its

beneficial tendency, and of the security and satisfaction it universally diffused. The cultivator, protected against all vexatious exac-
tions, and no longer at the beck of a tyrannical chief who made
unlimited demands upon his personal services, was beginning to
feel additional stimulants to his industry, to acquire a superior
relish for property, and to acknowledge that government and power
were not always the enemies of the lower ranks of society, or as
they modestly call themselves, *the little people* (*tiang-halit*). The
British administration of Java, with all its agents, having watched
the progress of the amended system at first with vigilant anxiety, at
last saw it nearly completed with success, and rejoiced in its beneficial operation on the prosperity, improvement, and happiness of
the people. During the two years that we retained possession of the
island, after the greatest part of its arrangements were carried into
effect, we had daily proofs of the amelioration they were producing.
The cultivation was extending, the influence of the chiefs appeared
to be progressively weakening, and the number of crimes, both
from the superior industry of the people now become interested in
the result of their labours, and from the contented tranquility produced by an increase of the means of subsistence, as well as from
the amended system of police . . . was gradually diminishing.

10. The Principles of the Culture System in Indonesia

*Unfortunately the new land rent system did not function so suc-
cessfully as Raffles imagined. It was introduced without adequate
surveys being made, and in such haste that many of its potential
advantages were lost. But convinced that the liberal principles of
colonial reform introduced by the British government were worthy
of further experimentation, the restored Dutch colonial administration confirmed them in 1817 in a modified form. Only when crippling drains on the government's financial resources occurred during the Java War of 1825 to 1830 did the Dutch regime move back
to some of the more basic principles of the past. Devised by Governor-General J. Count van den Bosch (1830 to 1833), a new cultivation, or "culture," system was introduced into Java in 1830 with*

the object of restoring the economic fortunes of the Dutch in In-
donesia. The following selection, taken from Clive Day's book,
The Policy and Administration of the Dutch in Java (The Mac-
millan Company, New York, 1904, pp. 247-250), gives an account
of the principles underlying the system. The assessments under the
new system were still, however, based on the earlier land rent as-
sessments.

The plan of [Johannes] Van den Bosch was confessedly a return
to the practices of the old East India Company. He reopened the
question, which had been so long debated, of the relative advantages
of forced and free cultures in Java. The character of the question
had changed as a result of the fiscal obligations into which the
East Indies had entered. The home government could no longer, as
formerly, afford to let the opposing parties fight it out at their
leisure, but must interfere to establish in the shortest possible time
the system which promised the best fiscal results. While the government recognized that under the scheme of the liberals, as represented by [Commissioner-General L. P. J. Viscount] Du Bus de
Ghisignies [1826 to 1830], the productive power of Java would increase, yet this could be but slowly and the government demanded
immediate returns. Van den Bosch had just returned from service
in the West Indies when he was consulted in the matter; he had
had there the opportunity to observe production by slave labor,
and was convinced that production in Java could never compete
with it so long as the Javanese were left free to cultivate as they
chose. When he was asked for his opinion in December, 1828, he
criticised the system of free cultures, and thought that "the institutions of the former East India Company, of which forced cultures
and deliveries were the chief pillars, deserved the preference."
Van den Bosch picked out all the weak points in the practical
working of the land-tax; he showed that it lent itself to abuse by
the native officials, and imposed on individual natives burdens
that were beyond their ability to bear. He asserted that under the
system of the land-tax forced services, instead of being alleviated,
were heavier than ever. He maintained that in the half century
ending in 1805, under the Company's system, there had not been a
serious political disturbance, while in the period from 1805 to

1830 there had been nine revolts or wars. Besides this comparison, which was not exact in the matter of fact, and which in any event did not justify the inference he suggested, he put another which made it seem that the natives preferred the districts of forced culture to those of the tax system. In reply to the advocates of free culture and colonization, he emphasized the amount of land held by the natives on a communal tenure and exaggerated the difficulties of securing export products from such land. It would be fruitless to review here all the arguments that he brought forward to justify a change of policy; they amounted to a general indictment of the tax system, which indeed offered material enough for criticism.

The plan of the culture system, as proposed by Van den Bosch in 1829, was in brief as follows: Instead of paying to the government a certain proportion of their crops, the natives were to put at its disposal a certain proportion of their land and labor-time. The revenue would then consist not in rice, which was almost universally cultivated and which was of comparatively little value to the government, but in export products grown under the direction of government contractors on the land set free by the remission of the former tax. According to the estimate, the natives would give up only one-fifth of their time in place of two-fifths of their main crop. The government proposed to bear the loss from failure of crops if this was not directly due to the fault of the cultivators, and moreover promised to pay the natives a certain small price for such amounts as they furnished. The government proposed in this way to secure products suited for export to the European market, on which it expected to realize profits largely in excess of the prices paid to natives and contractors, and of the costs of administration. To the natives it promised increased prosperity and a lighter burden of taxation, as a result of the fuller utilization of their chances under the far-sighted management of Europeans. The labor that before through carelessness and ignorance would have been wasted in idleness or in the cultivation of some cheap and superfluous crop was to supply a product of great value in the world market, and the natives were to share in the resulting profits. Van den Bosch justified his proposal not only by the benefits it would heap upon all parties, but by reference to previous history and the character of

left some entirely untouched. It is not necessary to defend here "equality of sacrifice" as a proper principle of taxation; whatever position one may take toward that principle, one will not defend such inequality of sacrifice as marked the application of the culture system.

12. Demarcation of British and Dutch Spheres of Influence in Southeast Asia in 1824

While the Dutch were involved in developing the economic resources of their colonial possessions in Southeast Asia, the British were establishing their foothold in Malaya. After taking possession of the island of Penang in the Malacca Straits in 1786, as well as a large slice of territory on the mainland opposite (Province Wellesley) fourteen years later, the unoccupied island of Singapore was acquired in 1819 by Sir Stamford Raffles from a Malay claimant to the old Johore empire. The subsequent "paper war" between the British and the Dutch on this subject led to the settlement of differences between the two nations in Southeast Asia by the conclusion of the Treaty of London in 1824, which recognized British rights to Singapore and agreed upon the Dutch cession of Malacca in exchange for the British colonial possessions in west Sumatra. From this time onwards, until the early 1840s when James Brooke's activities in Sarawak began to disturb the status quo, British and Dutch spheres of influence in Southeast Asia were generally demarcated and ultimately came to constitute the foundations of the existing national states of Malaysia, Singapore, and Indonesia. The following selection gives the main articles of the text of this important Treaty of 1824.

His Majesty The King of the United Kingdom of Great Britain and Ireland, and His Majesty The King of the Netherlands, desiring to place upon a footing, mutually beneficial, Their respective Possessions and the Commerce of Their Subjects in the East Indies, so that the welfare and prosperity of both Nations may be promoted, in all time to come, without those differences and jealousies which have, in former times, interrupted the harmony which ought always to subsist between Them; and being anxious that all occasions of misunderstanding between Their respective Agents may be, as much as possible, prevented . . . have agreed on the following Articles. . . .

ARTICLE II

The Subjects and Vessels of one Nation shall not pay, upon importation or exportation, at the Ports of the other in the Eastern Seas, any duty at a rate beyond the double of that at which the Subjects and Vessels of the Nation to which the Port belongs, are charged.

The Duties paid on exports or imports at a British Port, on the Continent of India, or in Ceylon, on Dutch bottoms, shall be arranged so as, in no case, to be charged at more than double the amount of the duties paid by British Subjects, and on British bottoms.

In regard to any article upon which no duty is imposed, when imported or exported by the Subjects, or on the Vessels, of the Nation to which the Port belongs, the duty charged upon the Subjects or Vessels of the other, shall, in no case, exceed six per cent.

ARTICLE III

The High Contracting Parties engage, that no Treaty hereafter made by Either, with any Native Power in the Eastern Seas, shall contain any Article tending, either expressly, or by the imposition of unequal duties, to exclude the Trade of the other Party from the Ports of such Native Power: and that if, in any Treaty now existing on either Part, any Article to that effect has been admitted, such Article shall be abrogated upon the conclusion of the present Treaty. . . .

ARTICLE IV

Their Britannick and Netherland Majesties engage to give strict Orders, as well as to Their Civil and Military Authorities, as to Their Ships of War, to respect the Freedom of Trade, established by Articles I, II and III; and, in no case, to impede a free communication of the Natives in the Eastern Archipelago, with the Ports of the Two Governments, respectively, or of the Subjects of the Two Governments with the Ports belonging to Native Powers. . . .

ARTICLE VI

It is agreed that Orders shall be given by the Two Governments to Their Officers and Agents in the East, not to form any new Settlement on any of the Islands in the Eastern Seas, without previous Authority from their respective Governments in Europe.

ARTICLE VII

The Molucca Islands, and especially Amboyna, Banda, Ternate, and their immediate Dependencies, are excepted from the operation of the I, II, III, and IV Articles, until the Netherland Government shall think fit to abandon the monopoly of Spices; but if the said Government shall, at any time previous to such abandonment of the monopoly, allow the Subjects of any Power, other than a Native Asiatic Power, to carry on any Commercial Intercourse with the said Islands, the Subjects of His Britannick Majesty shall be admitted to such Intercourse, upon a footing precisely similar. . . .

ARTICLE IX

The Factory of Fort Marlborough [Benkulen[1]], and all the English Possessions on the Island of Sumatra, are hereby ceded to His Netherland Majesty: and His Britannick Majesty further engages that no British Settlement shall be formed on that Island, nor any Treaty concluded by British Authority, with any Native Prince, Chief, or State therein.

ARTICLE X

The Town and Fort of Malacca, and its Dependencies, are hereby ceded to His Britannick Majesty; and His Netherland Majesty en-

[1] See Selection 6.

gages, for Himself and his Subjects, never to form any Establishment on any part of the Peninsula of Malacca, or to conclude any
Treaty with any Native Prince, Chief, or State therein. . . .

ARTICLE XII

His Netherland Majesty withdraws the objections which have
been made to the occupation of the Island of Singapore, by the
Subjects of His Britannick Majesty.

His Britannick Majesty, however, engages, that no British Establishment shall be made on the Carimon Isles, or on the Islands
of Battam, Bintang, Lingen, or on any of the other Islands South
of the Straits of Singapore, nor any Treaty concluded by British
Authority with the Chiefs of those Islands. . . .

13. Early British Rule in Upper Burma

*In the same year that the Treaty of London resolved Anglo-Dutch
differences in maritime Southeast Asia, Great Britain became involved in armed conflict with the mainland state of Burma. Under
her vigorous ruler Bodawpaya (1782 to 1819), Burma's territories
were extended to include Arakan, which made her frontiers con-
terminous with those of British India. British missions despatched
to the Court of Ava in the late eighteenth and early nineteenth
centuries failed to resolve border problems, and Anglo-Burmese
relations deteriorated seriously after 1811 when an Arakanese rebel,
operating with a force recruited in British India, entered Arakan
and seized Mrohaung. Despite assurances that the rebels were not
receiving British support, Burma threatened to invade Chittagong,
and only the death of the rebel leader in 1815 temporarily relieved
the situation. In 1817 Burmese forces invaded Assam, and the governor appointed by the new ruler of Burma, Bagyidaw (1819 to
1837), brought increasing pressure to bear on the British frontier.
Finally, in 1823 the Burmese seized Shapuri island on the British
side of the Naaf estuary, and early in the following year the massing
of Burmese troops for a march on Chittagong led to a British declaration of war. After a two years' period of hostilities, Burma fi-*

nally agreed to British demands for the cession of Arakan, Tenas-
serim, and Assam, together with the payment of an indemnity of
one million pounds sterling, about one-thirteenth of the total Brit-
ish war debt.

Anglo-Burmese relations did not much improve during the fol-
lowing years. The British Residency provided by the Treaty of
Yandabo (1826) was withdrawn from Ava in 1840, and a series of in-
cidents during the next decade led to a renewal of hostilities in
1852. The British invasion of Burma resulted in a palace revolution
engineered by the "peace" party and led to the elevation to the
throne of King Mindon; but British annexation of Pegu at the end
of 1852 proved a stumbling block to peace, and, although hostilities
ceased in 1853 and were never resumed, a formal treaty was not
concluded by the Burmese. Pegu was a bone in the throat of Ava
and prevented an early restitution of normal relations between the
two powers. When, moreover, shortly after his elevation to the
throne in 1878, King Thibaw began to interfere in the affairs of
the British-controlled Bombay-Burma Trading Corporation, this
provided sufficient cause for the British, alarmed as they were by
the possible extension of French influence from Indo-China, to de-
mand not only the submission of the Trading Corporation dispute
to arbitration, but also the virtual control of Burma's foreign rela-
tions. Thibaw's resistance to these demands met swift retribution.
After a lightning campaign lasting two weeks, he was taken
prisoner in his palace at Mandalay on November 28, 1885, and Up-
per Burma was formally annexed by the British and united with
Lower Burma as a province of the Indian Empire.

The following selection, taken from Professor D. G. E. Hall's
short history of Burma *(Hutchinson's University Library, London,*
1950, pp. 142-146), gives some account of the establishment of Brit-
ish rule in Upper Burma, and its effects. Reprinted by permission.

The abolition of the Ava kingship and the formal annexation of
Upper Burma on 1 January, 1886, presented the British with far
bigger problems than the earlier annexations had brought. The
first question to be decided was whether the new territory should
form a protected state like Afghanistan or be brought directly under British administration. Lord Dufferin, the [British-India] Vice-

roy, favoured the former solution, but it was found to be impracticable. The Hlutdaw [Supreme Burmese Council] was discredited, there was no suitable candidate able to maintain himself without British military assistance, and the country was too disorganized. So after a meeting between Lord Dufferin and Sir Frederick Roberts, the Commander-in-Chief, at Mandalay in February 1886, direct administration was decided on. Sir Charles Bernard became Chief Commissioner for the whole of Burma, the Hlutdaw was abolished, and a consultative body of former ministers was set up. . . .

The most urgent problem was that of disorder. Notwithstanding the fact that when the question of military operations against [King] Thibaw had originally been discussed, Major-General Knox Gore had estimated that while only 500 men would be required to take Mandalay, ten times that number, in addition to the already reinforced Burma garrison, would be needed for the task of 'pacification,' many people, including the [British] Viceroy himself, had optimistically believed that the Burmese would welcome the 'coming of the Great Queen.' The Burmese army, however, refused to obey the order to surrender and carried on widespread guerrilla warfare. . . . There was even a serious rebellion in Lower Burma. It took five years of hard campaigning to quell the resistance. The situation became so grave during the later months of 1886 that Sir Frederick Roberts had to transfer his quarters from India to Burma from November 1886 to February 1887, and an army of 32,000 troops and 8500 military police was fully engaged.

For civil administration Upper Burma was divided into fourteen districts each under a Deputy or Assistant Commissioner with a Police Assistant. So far as revenue and civil justice were concerned, the original intention was for these to work through indigenous local agencies according to local methods. As in Lower Burma local administration was based on the circle with its hereditary headman, the taikthugyi, or, as he was more often known in Upper Burma, myothugyi. But Bernard's successor, Sir Charles Crosthwaite, who came with firmly fixed ideas of Indian administration, brought with him a draft scheme for breaking up the circles into villages. He thought that the degree of power exercised by thugyis, and the absence of village communities with recognized heads, were defects which should be remedied.

The rebellious state of the country played into his hands, since the thugyis were the chief leaders of resistance in Upper Burma, and had failed to suppress it in Lower Burma. The upshot of it all was the conversion of the village into an administrative unit by the Upper Burma Village Regulation of 1887 and the Burma Village Act of 1889. These two measures imposed statutory duties concerning the maintenance of order and the collection of revenue upon the headman and villagers.

It was some time before the evil results of the new system began to show themselves, since the circle headmen were only gradually abolished. [J. S.] Furnivall, from his long experience of administration in Burma, examines them with much acumen. He writes that in the first place the villages had duties without any compensating rights imposed upon them. In the second place in order to combine adequate emoluments for the headmen with efficient administration, a comprehensive scheme of amalgamation had to be carried through after 1909. The merging of villages which ensued, and led to a reduction in the number of headmen by over 2000, made the 'village' a mere artificial administrative unit. In the third place with the disappearance of the circle headman the habit of referring serious disputes between adjacent villages to his arbitration "so as to arrive at a compromise according to known custom" tended to die out, and "the mechanical logic of the law courts" was substituted. "The popular self-government of Burmese times was replaced by a foreign legal system," he comments. Whether the semi-feudal power of the myothugyi is rightly termed 'popular self-government', and further, whether it would have been possible to develop the circle system of Burmese times into an institution capable of carrying out the new duties necessarily imposed by twentieth-century conditions, are somewhat debatable questions, it might seem. Burma unfortunately possessed no institution similar to the Javanese *desa* [village] upon which a healthy local administration could have been based. . . .

Stress has been laid upon the importance of the Buddhist Church in Burmese life. Burma was *par excellence* a Buddhist state. From the earliest days of annexation this situation was clearly recognized by the British and, save under the stress of actual warfare, all possible respect was shown to sacred places and religious observances. When, in the early days of the occupation of Tenasserim, the monks complained that a monastic building was being used as an armoury, it was restored to them. No attempt was ever made to undermine the religion of the people. British policy was that of *laissez faire,* so long as religious practice did not clash with the maintenance of law and order.

This negative attitude, inevitable as it was under the circumstances, had unfortunate results. The monastic establishment cut off from its headquarters at the capital, suffered in both discipline and cohesion. After the annexation of Pegu in 1852[,] the deterioration became more strongly marked, since at first there was a considerable exodus to Upper Burma, and many monasteries were deserted. Later on, when large numbers of people returned, many monks remained behind in the Kingdom of Ava, and there was little attempt to restore the monasteries which had fallen out of use. The census of 1891 shows that whereas under Burmese rule every Lower Burma village had its monastery, there was then only one to every three or four villages.

Perhaps the chief cause of decay was the British refusal to give official recognition to the Buddhist ecclesiastical code on the grounds that this would constitute the kind of interference with religion, which the [British] Queen's Declaration of 1858 at the close of the Indian Mutiny had forbidden. It meant in practice that the power of the Buddhist authorities to maintain discipline almost disappeared. In 1884, when Colonel (later Sir Edward) Sladen was consulted regarding the possible effects of the annexation of Thibaw's Kingdom, he said that he hoped the mistake made in Pegu would not be repeated in Upper Burma, and urged that government should support the lawful authority of the heads of the Buddhist Church.

After the deposition of Thibaw, however, his advice went unheeded, notwithstanding strong pressure from responsible Burmese leaders. . . . Three matters were involved, endowments, the holding of examinations in the Pali scriptures, and discipline. There was no difficulty over the first two; but [there was] over the third. . . .

[J. S.] Furnivall sums up the resulting situation thus: "For some years ecclesiastical causes were left for decision by the Order, but judicial decisions gradually brought them within the jurisdiction of the civil courts. In ecclesiastical, as in lay affairs, British law supplanted Burmese custom, the last vestige of a monastic autonomy disappeared, and with them the only effective machinery for regulating admission to the Order and expelling disreputable members."

The years that followed were to see the gradual disintegration of the Order, and the monks, who had at one time been the cultural leaders of the people, tended to become, though with many notable exceptions, an ignorant, disorderly class, preaching sedition and creating unrest.

14. Reasons for British Intervention in Malaya

Great Britain had been able to act decisively in Burma in 1885 without fear of reaction by France because of the latter's own heavy involvement in Indo-China. It has been argued, in fact, that Britain acted with decision in Burma in order to prevent a later conflict with France for hegemony in Southeast Asia. Certainly a decade earlier Lord Kimberley, the British Colonial Secretary, had expressed the basic motive for British intervention in the Malay Peninsula in these terms, though in this instance the power referred to was Germany: ". . . we could not see with indifference," he wrote, "interference of foreign Powers in the affairs of the Peninsula, on the other hand it is difficult to see how we should be justified in objecting to the native [Malay] States seeking aid elsewhere if we refuse to take any steps to remedy the evils [of disorder] complained of." The following selection gives an analysis of British intervention in Malaya during the 1870s based upon this general hypothesis of British fear of foreign intervention and is extracted from Professor C. D. Cowan's book, Nineteenth-Century Malaya: The Origins of British Political Control *(Oxford University Press,*

London, 1961, pp. 169-175) by permission of the author and publishers.

Reasoning from the Colonial Office papers we . . . reach the conclusion that the decision to take some action in Malaya, and if necessary to intervene in the affairs of the states, was provoked not by conditions in the Peninsula, nor by any consideration of British economic interests there, but by fear of foreign intervention. This is confirmed by the terms in which Kimberley justified his instructions to Sir Andrew Clarke [Governor of the Straits Settlements] to [W. E.] Gladstone, [the Prime Minister]:

> The condition of the Malay Peninsula [he wrote] is becoming very serious. It is the old story of misgovernment of Asiatic States. This might go on without any very serious consequences except the stoppage of trade, were it not that European and Chinese capitalists, stimulated by the great riches in tin mines which exist in some of the Malay States are suggesting to the native Princes that they should seek the aid of Europeans to enable them to put down the disorders which prevail. We are the paramount power on the Peninsula up to the limit of the States, tributary to Siam, and looking to the vicinity of India[,] and our whole position in the East[,] I apprehend that it would be a serious matter if any other European Power were to obtain a footing in the Peninsula.

This attitude was consistent with the continuing theme of British policy in Malaya and Indonesia. . . . It was in line with the idea that the promotion of British economic interests in the area, however desirable in itself, has in fact always been secondary to the defence of India, the protection of the sea route to China, and the denial of bases along that route to potentially dangerous powers.

Many interesting questions arise from this conclusion, but we can only find space to discuss two of them here. First, what led Kimberley to conclude that the threat of foreign intervention in Malaya was real enough to justify action? Of the other Colonial Powers Holland was precluded by the Treaty of 1824[1] from interfering, and a general colonial settlement had been reached with her only two years before with the Sumatra and Gold Coast Treaties of 1871. France was prostrate after her war with Prussia, and her

---

[1] See Selection 12.

colonial activities were to remain at a stand-still until after the Congress of Berlin in 1878. In the East after the Franco-Siamese Settlement of 1867 secured the recognition of the French protectorate over Cambodia[2] successive French Consuls at Bangkok contented themselves with the administration of their extra-territorial rights in Siam. So little were any other states regarded as potential rivals in London that a large concession in North Borneo granted to the American Consul in Brunei in 1865 passed almost unnoticed in the Foreign Office and Colonial Office records. Even a Prussian attempt to survey Blair Harbour, on the east coast of Johore, and the off-lying islands, for use as a coaling station during the Franco-Prussian War was not taken very seriously in London.

By the middle of 1873 however conditions had changed. A Dutch invasion of the Atjeh [in north Sumatra] at the beginning of the year created a focus of unsettlement in the Straits. The Atjehnese leaders, seeking a counter-balance against the Dutch, attempted to obtain the support of some other Power by offering island bases and trading monopolies. Rumours of secret treaties negotiated with the United States and the Italian consuls in Singapore were denied by the countries concerned, but they were taken seriously enough in London to engage the attention of the British Cabinet. Italy and the United States were not the only 'new nations' which had to be considered . . . and though a junior Colonial Office official remarked that the prospect of a German protectorate was small the Liberal ministers were not so certain that they might not meet with trouble from this quarter.

There had been a marked change in the British attitude towards Germany during the course of the Franco-Prussian War, which transferred from France to Germany political predominance in Europe. One feature of the uncertainty which followed this disruption of the balance of power was an invasion scare in England, prompted by the publication in 1871 of an anonymous pamphlet, *The Battle of Dorking*. Another was a series of alarming rumours started by the King of the Belgians, who sent warnings to his English friends of an understanding between Russia, Germany, France and the United States to act together in support of Russia

[2] See Selection 18.

against England in Asia. The Liberal ministers were not much impressed by the invasion scare, and Gladstone commented acidly on the warnings from Belgium—'This intelligence rather tends to lower my estimate of the *acumen* of the King of the Belgians.' But they had some basis in fact; the years after 1870 saw a drawing together of Germany and Russia as part of the Bismarckian alliance system, which was consolidated in June 1873 by the creation of the *Dreikaiserbund* between Germany, Russia and Austria. Bismarck's support had already enabled Russia in 1870 to denounce with impunity those clauses of the Treaty of Paris (1856) which forbade her to maintain military or naval establishments on the Black Sea. Russia was Britain's most feared rival in Asia, and in the years between 1866 and 1872 her conquest of the Khanates of Central Asia brought her to the boundaries of Afghanistan and enabled her to intensify her pressure on Persia. Both Britain's traditional opposition to any power which aspired to the domination of Europe, and her suspicion of Russia therefore urged her to view with suspicion any hint of the acquisition of territory by Germany.

There is no indication in any of the official papers that in 1873 any minister or official servant of the Crown had knowledge that any other Power actually contemplated the acquisition of territory or influence in Malaya. The consolidation of the British position there seems to have served rather to remove temptation than to forestall a projected movement in that direction. The background to Kimberley's decision is by no means clear, and it remains for some future student of this period to uncover definite evidence of the circumstances which prompted him to take the view he did. It is just possible, in view of events in Fiji and the Gold Coast at this time, that he justified intervention in Malaya in these terms because he thought that no other argument would secure the acquiescence of Gladstone. But until evidence to the contrary is forthcoming the only course is to accept at its face value Kimberley's own declaration that:

> Her Majesty's Government could not see with indifference the interference of a foreign Power in the affairs of the Peninsula, and it would be difficult to justify an objection to the Native States applying for aid to other Powers if the British Government refuses to lend its aid.

We come now to the second question for discussion. Granted that some move must be made in Malaya, what should it be, annexation or the proclamation of Protectorates? Again there is little evidence that bears directly on the question. One course of action seems to have been ruled out from the beginning. There was never any prospect of the Liberal Government sanctioning annexation. Two similar problems with which the Liberals were faced in 1873, in the Gold Coast and Fiji, did end in annexation. But the deed was done not by the Liberals but their Conservative successors. In the Gold Coast the Ashanti War was still in progress when the Liberals quitted office early in 1874, and it was left to their successors to annex the old 'Proctectorate'. In Fiji, where the activities of 'black-birders', traders and adventurers kept the islands in turmoil, the Gladstone Government was again faced with the need for action. Both the settlers and the natives pressed for annexation. Kimberley continually urged the reluctant Gladstone to a decision, but in June 1873 the Cabinet fell back on the expedient of a Commission of Enquiry, which staved off responsibility long enough to get the tottering Liberal ministry out of office.

It is tempting to see Kimberley's instructions to Sir Andrew Clarke to 'enquire and report' as an application of Fijian tactics to Malaya. But several circumstances combine to suggest that they were not intended to shelve or delay action, and were not the result of a politically inspired compromise. In the first place the original suggestion came from the Permanent Secretary at the Colonial Office, [Sir Robert] Herbert, who wrote:

> As Sir A. Clarke is believed to be able and cautious in administrative matters it might be well to desire him confidentially to consider after his arrival whether it would be safe [and] advantageous to extend our influence to some parts of the Malay territories beyond our own Settlements.

In the second place Clarke's instructions were never submitted in draft to any other department of state. Kimberley recorded in his original minute of 22 July [1873] his intention of speaking to [Lord] Granville at the Foreign Office and [the Duke of] Argyll at the India Office on the subject, and may have done so. But when detailed memoranda on the situation in Malaya prepared by his

officials were presented to him, he realized that under the arrangement reached in 1868 he was entitled to conduct relations with the
states not under Siamese influence without reference to the Foreign
Office, and insisted on doing so. Lastly, neither Clarke's instructions
nor the general situation in Malaya appear ever to have formed the
subject of discussion in Cabinet. There is no reference to Malaya
in Gladstone's Cabinet minutes. The Liberal Cabinet during 1873
were distracted by continual domestic crises, and what time they
had for colonial affairs was occupied by Fiji and Ashanti. Clarke's
instructions were therefore entirely the work of Kimberley and
his officials, and it was not until 10 September [1873] that the draft
despatch embodying these instructions was submitted to Gladstone.
He returned it without comment.

The instructions in their final and now widely known form were
somewhat weaker than the draft. But this seems to have been the
result of purely accidental circumstances. From the beginning, as
a result of Herbert's suggestion and the departmental memoranda
on existing treaties with the Malay States, Kimberley had had in
mind an extension of these treaties so as to allow of increased British
influence in the affairs of the states, and to exclude the possibility
that any other Power might establish itself there. This followed
naturally from the nature of the existing treaties. When these were
subjected to detailed scrutiny in the Colonial Office it was realized
for the first time that Perak, for instance, was almost a British
Protectorate already, as [a] result of the 1826 treaties. Thus the
draft instructions called on Clarke to report 'what mode of proceed-
ing should in his opinion be adopted', making it quite clear that some
form of action was in any case going to be taken, since 'the interests
of the British Settlements require that we shall exert our influence
to put an end to the state of anarchy and disorder which prevails'.
These instructions were originally drawn up in the form of a con-
fidential letter to be given to Clarke before he sailed for Malaya.
But probably owing to the time the papers were kept by Gladstone
the letter was not ready when Clarke sailed, and it had to be turned
into a despatch. It seems to have been this that resulted in the instructions being toned down, and in the passage which dealt with
'the interference of a foreign Power in the affairs of the Peninsula'
being cut out. The operative part of the instructions then read:

I have to request you will carefully ascertain as far as you are able the actual condition of affairs in each state, and that you will report to me whether there are, in your opinion, any steps which can properly be taken by the Colonial Government to promote the restoration of peace and order, and to secure protection to trade and commerce with the Native Territories.

I would wish you especially to consider whether it would be advisable to appoint a British officer to reside in any of the States. Such an appointment could of course only be made with the full consent of the Native Government and the expenses connected with it would have to be defrayed by the Government of the Straits Settlements.

To sum up, the decision to depart from the policy of rigid non-interference in Malaya was prompted by fear that if the disordered conditions in some of the states were not ended some other Power might be invited to intervene. This decision was taken by the Secretary of State on his own initiative. He and his officials had in mind an extension of the existing treaties with Perak and Selangor which would eliminate the possibility of foreign interference. They also envisaged the possibility that British Agents might be stationed in these states, but they did not elaborate this suggestion. Instead they decided that as a first step the new Governor of the Straits Settlements should be asked to report on the practicability of these proposals.

4

DIFFERENTIAL PATTERN
OF COLONIAL RULE
IN SOUTHEAST ASIA

The Dutch forward movement in north Sumatra, which was designed to incorporate the sultanate of Achin within the formal bonds of colonial administration, and the extension between 1857 and 1873 of French influence in Indo-China provided, in British eyes, ample justification for the political action taken in the Malay states in the mid-1870s. Although disclaiming all intention of annexation, the British bound the Malay rulers of Perak, Selangor, and Sungei Ujong to acept the "advice" of British residents on all matters except those touching upon Malay religion and custom. Control of the collection of revenue was regulated under the advice of the residents, and this meant that practically the whole of the administration of the states was placed in British hands, as the collection and control of the revenues and the tendering of advice which had to be acted upon covered all branches of executive authority. A decade later France obliged the Cambodian ruler to accept French direction in internal administration by undertaking to "enact all the administrative, judicial, financial and commercial reforms which the French government judges necessary in the interest of the Protectorate." The entire civil service was placed under a Chief French Resident.

It is impossible in a few words to attempt to summarize the different ways in which the Western colonial powers ruled their territorial possessions in Southeast Asia during the nineteenth and twentieth centuries. The best approach has therefore been to make selections which are generally descriptive of the systems of rule within each country of Southeast Asia. Selections 15 through 17 have been taken from books which reflect to some degree a procolonial point of view. An attempt is made to redress the balance by Selections 18 and 19, which are more critical of the colonial governments and their systems of administration.

15. Dutch Colonial Rule in Indonesia

The following selection is taken from a semiofficial Dutch publication of 1945 under the title Mission Interrupted: The Dutch in the East Indies and their Work in the XXth Century (*Elsevier, Amsterdam, 1945, pp. 217-225*). *Reprinted by permission.*

It should . . . be remembered that the Dutch had gone to the Indies in order to trade and not to found an empire. Compelled by circumstances to exercise actual rule from the first they adopted the principle to leave the inhabitants as much as possible under their own rulers. This meant that in many regions they actually remained under their own princes while in regions placed under direct Dutch rule native chieftains were used wherever possible. According to the same principle for Chinese and Arabs "officers" of these respective nationalities were appointed.

In a society of this type a centralised government was indicated. It was exercised to the remotest corners by civil servants appointed as his representatives by the Governor-General and responsible to him. These civil servants thus acquired such intimate knowledge of the indigenous population as no one else could attain. The Civil Service decreed what was good or ill for the population, what it needed or what it could do without, what burdens could be laid upon its shoulders. The Civil Service did not only exercise complete rule over the population, but it also was its daily judge, it watched over the health of men and beasts, it looked after the interests of agriculture and cattle-breeding. There was no government concern that was not either entirely in the hands of the Civil Service or greatly influenced by it.

Various circumstances brought about a gradual change of this simple structure. At the beginning of the XXth century the Netherlands came to realise their moral duty with regard to the Indies and the Indonesians. The direct result was a considerable extension and intensification of the government's activities in the interest of the population. It was a fortunate circumstance that increasing revenues were able to meet the increase of expenditure entailed by this extension; also that the Awakening of the East penetrated into the archipelago thus creating for the measures taken the possibility to come to fruition. As a rule the initiative to ever greater activity [in] new fields of Governmental interest was taken by the Civil Service. As these interests gradually developed, special services with experts were created with a strictly centralised organisation.

The history of the East Indian governmental system in the last forty years [down till the Second World War] is dominated by the question how to find the most efficient forms for carrying out a governing task so greatly changed in character. Expanding beyond all expectation it overburdened the central government so that a partial transfer of responsibilities was necessary. This might have been brought about by granting lower officials a greater measure of independence in carrying out certain policies but, as it happened, the course of events was different.

The centripetal tendencies of the special services had awakened a desire in local residents to have a say in matters affecting their town or region. The idea of local councils began to take shape.

So, from 1905 on, a number of municipalities were organised. This was followed in 1918 by the creation of a central representative body, called the Volksraad (People's Council), at first with an advisory character only but from 1927 on invested with co-legislative powers. Finally, from 1925 on, the territory was divided into provinces and "governments". . . .

According to the Netherlands' constitution the supreme authority over the Indies was vested in the Queen. Considerable influence however was exercised by Parliament. Not only did its co-legislative powers extend to legislation pertaining to the Indies but the Minister of Colonies (the colonial secretary of state) appointed by the Queen was responsible to it. He was able to bear this responsibility because the Governor-General, also appointed by the Queen in whose name he exercised the general government of the East Indies, for all his actions was responsible to the Minister of Colonies. This implied that the Governor-General had to heed all rulings of the Minister of Colonies in matters of government and legislation. The seemingly wellnigh dictatorial power of the Governor-General was therefore narrowly limited by the effective interference of the Minister of Colonies and by the democratic governmental system of the mother country.

The Governor-General was assisted by a Council of the Netherlands East Indies whose advice in all important matters it was mandatory for him to seek and in certain specific cases he could only act in full agreement with that Council.

Legislation of the East Indies relative to internal affairs was effected by the Governor-General in agreement with the central representative body, the Volksraad. The budget, in so far as agreement had been reached between the Governor-General and the Volksraad was provisionally fixed by the Governor-General, subject to definitive approval by Parliament in Holland. Lacking the required agreement in legislative matters even after repeated debate in the Volksraad, the Governor-General could request the Minister of Colonies to promulgate the disputed ordinance or, in case of urgency, do so himself. Such cases, though comparatively rare, always attracted an inordinate amount of attention whenever they occurred.

The Volksraad met in two sessions with a combined duration of four months. The briefness of these sessions had the advantage that members were able to keep on in their normal functions and thus did not lose contact with social life. Since on the other hand a co-legislative body cannot be spared during eight months of the year, a Committee of Delegates was instituted, consisting of one fourth of the total membership and chosen by the Volksraad itself. This Committee, with the sole exception of the discussion of the budget, enjoyed the same powers as the council-in-pleno. Mutual friction between the two bodies was prevented by certain measures found quite satisfactory in practice.

In composing the membership of the Council consisting of 61 members care was taken that the diversity of population groups was reflected as much as possible. About one half of the total number of seats was allotted to Dutchmen, and there was a fixed allocation of some seats to Chinese and Arabs. A division of the native population into a number of electoral districts took care of the interests of the different nationalities according to their relative importance. Since half the members (Dutch, native or Chinese) were elected and the other half directly nominated by the Governor-General, it was possible to meet widely diverging desires and needs.

It may be said that a considerable part of the Government's responsibility was, in this way, transferred from [T]he Hague to Batavia. This does not mean that the relationship between Holland and the East Indies was settled to everybody's satisfaction. In practice there still remained moot points requiring further attention. The Indies insisted especially that internal affairs should indeed be left to the East Indian Government bodies and that the East Indian budget, discussed in the Volksraad with minute expert care, be fixed directly in the East Indies in so far as agreement between Governor-General and Volksraad had been reached. Thus would be reserved for discussion by the States-General at The Hague those parts of the budget and those East Indian ordinances about which no such agreement had been reached, as well as bills of law touching the joint interests of Holland and the East Indies or those of the Kingdom of the Netherlands as such. . . .

On the one hand the authorities' wish for greater efficiency, on the other that of the inhabitants to collaborate in the government from 1925 on led to the so-called Administrative Reform, that is to say the organisation of provinces and "governments". This Reform worked out quite differently on Java and on the Outer Islands.

On Java 3 provinces were organised, subdivided into about 70 regencies and a few score of municipalities. These provinces, as regards their relationship to the central government and the regencies and municipalities under them, were copied on the model of the Dutch provinces. These however had a historic growth; those in Java were artificially created and, moreover, each comprised an area larger than the whole of the Netherlands and numbered respectively 12, 12 and 16 million inhabitants! The chances of vitality were made as favourable as possible. West-Java with its

Sundanese population formed an ethnic unity, but the boundaries between Central and East-Java were arbitrarily fixed mainly because the territory would otherwise have been too unwieldly for one province. To these provinces a large task was immediately assigned and later this task was even still more enlarged. They were also equipped with adequate personnel and never were seriously harassed by financial troubles.

To the political collaboration of the inhabitants was given due scope by the organisation of Provincial Councils of more than 50 members, in which a certain number of seats were allotted to each of the three groups of Dutchmen, Indonesians and Chinese. Each of these groups was represented also in the Executive Board. It can hardly be said that the population showed much enthusiasm over these councils; they were entirely beyond the sphere of interest of the ordinary folk. Of the more educated people, some were indifferent; others recognised the utility of these councils.

It is a different matter with the autonomous regencies. This reform was much more hazardous. With a few exceptions the Regencies were historical territorial units and the population was fully conscious of belonging to a certain Regency. This however does not mean that they had any idea of the Regency as an autonomous organisation.

It was by no means certain that the Regent would be equal to his new task. After 1912 some responsibilities of Dutch officials had gradually been shifted to native Regents in order to "de-guardianise" him, as it was called. Now by the Administrative Reform Law all of a sudden this emancipation was applied to all Regents to whom, at the same time, was given the difficult task of presiding over the newly created Regency-Councils. . . .

Though the task of Provinces and Regencies did not yet by any means come to its fullest expansion, it may already be said that the administrative reform on Java actually did bring relief to the central Government and the central services. In each province provincial services were organised with their own staff of experts to take over the task of the central departments. In education, irrigation, building and repair of roads, agricultural advice, forestry etc.[,] a large part of the work was transferred to the provincial services. The central services however retained the supervision of the general interests for the whole of the East Indies and the decisions entailing questions of principle.

This devolution was not only applied to the provincial services, but as much as possible local interests were transferred to the Regencies under the supervision of the provincial government. The Regencies in turn organised separate services. In this way measures formerly decreed from one central point were adapted as much as possible to local needs.

In an even greater measure transfer of responsibility took place in the case of the municipalities organised from 1905 on. In their organisation they entirely copied the Dutch municipal law. The responsibilities entrusted to them at first were slight; only slowly did they succeed in gaining more say in administrative affairs. The civil servants and the special services, conscious of a good record, were not in a hurry to shed some of their responsibilities to green-horns. They rather regarded municipalities as "western enclaves in an oriental country" and did not permit them to have anything to do with the affairs of natives living within the municipality. These remained under their own chiefs or under the Civil Service. The larger part of the municipal area, the native kampongs [villages], thus fell outside the scope of municipal activity. It took far too long before this theoretical question was solved in favour of the munic-ipalities. It cannot be denied that the kampong population was greatly benefited by the work of the municipality, though the problem of kampong improvement that would devour millions of florins was not yet solved.

The administrative reform of the Outer Islands had quite a dif-ferent character. The diversity of peoples, differing in customs, standard of education and political habits, made it impossible to copy there the reform introduced on Java. Opinions differed on the manner of reform. Meanwhile the first steps were taken in 1938 by the organisation of three "governments": Sumatra, Borneo and "the Great East" being the eastern part of the Archipelago, each under a governor. Autonomous group-communes were to be es-tablished under these governments, not, like those on Java, all of a pattern, but area and responsibility for each one was to be fixed separately. Within a few years these governments were to be trans-formed into provinces, that is to say councils were to be adjoined to the governors and their responsibilities were to be fixed separately. The tendency towards uniformity here remained a menace to the best intentions.

On the whole the form of government-by-discussion, embodied in the councils, was found satisfactory. The councils, whether of province, regency or municipality, always had the decisive vote. The governor, regent or burgomaster could only suspend a decision and refer it to a higher authority for annulment.

The manner of representation was different for the different councils and groups of the population. The principle followed was not that every adult had the right to cast his vote for a representative, but that the best possible representation should be found for the heterogeneous East Indian society. The electoral systems were changed repeatedly as circumstances demanded. Moreover it was felt that elections alone did not give sufficient guarantee for the best representation. Party system was still little developed and it was obvious that many suitable persons would not be willing to stand for election so that certain groups might not be represented at all. This difficulty was solved by direct nomination of about one third of the total membership. Though it would be an overstatement to say that these nominations were always universally applauded, there never was serious dissatisfaction. The principal grievances were concerned with the nominations in Regency Councils, since the members of those councils (and of the Municipal Councils) were electors of the Provincial Councils and the Volksraad. Thus the direct nomination of electors met with more opposition than that of representatives! When . . . it was proposed by the electoral reform committee to introduce this system of partial nomination also for the Municipal Councils, this proposal was supported by the Volksraad.

The political division of the Dutch East Indies is not so simple that a subdivision of the entire territory into 6 provinces (3 on Java . . . 3 on the Outer Islands) and of these in turn into regencies and municipalities (or group-communes and municipalities on the Outer Islands) should suffice. On the contrary: such a division leaves out a very large part of the territory, that is to say the autonomous native states. On Java there are four autonomous states, the chief of which are Jocjakarta and Surakarta, numbering 1½ and 2½ million inhabitants. On the Outer Islands their area comprises more than half the territory. They vary in importance and size from a village to a minor Dutch province and the level of their civilisation varies greatly. When [Dutch] administration in the Outer Islands was intensified, it was impossible to leave these states alone. Not all their princes and rulers however were able to direct the necessary dvelopment and there was little hope that education could soon make them equal to that task. In the last decades before the war the constant urge to stimulate the development of native society often led to more interference with the internal affairs of the native states than was originally intended. This was made possible by the terms of the treaties concluded with the native princes. For practical reasons some of the native states were even abolished: in 1914 there were 340, in 1930 only 273. From that date on there was a reaction in the policy of the Government aiming at greater development of the autonomous administration, and even leading to the restoration of some abolished states. In this new policy they were regarded as free forms of decentralisation also fit to take over their share of the Central Government's task. The measure in which the native population might be given a voice depended on the existing political structure and the possibility of democratising it, perhaps in an Indonesian democratic spirit.

16. British Colonial Rule in Malaya

The next selection has been taken from a book first published in 1944 by one of the greatest British scholars of Malaya, the late Sir Richard Winstedt, entitled Britain and Malaya 1786-1948 *(Longmans, Green and Co. Ltd., London, revised edtion, 1949, pp. 36-46). (Reprinted by permission of Her Majesty's Stationery Office, London.) The selection describes the basic pattern of British rule in Malaya down to the fall of the country to the Japanese in 1941.*

Before its fall, Malaya, a country about the size of England, was a piece of political joinery "crossly indented and whimsically dovetailed" out of three types of constitution.

(a) The Straits Settlements (comprising the island of Singapore, the island of Penang with Province Wellesley, and the settlement of Malacca) were a British possession, from 1867 a Crown Colony. All of them had been purchased from Malay rulers except Malacca which had been transferred to [Great Britain] by the Dutch,[1] who in 1641 had conquered it from the Portuguese who had captured it in 1511.[2]

(b) Perak, Selangor, Negri Sembilan and Pahang, coming under British protection by treaties with their Rulers in the seventies and eighties of the nineteenth century, had been the Federated Malay States since 1895.

(c) Johore, Kedah, Perlis, Kelantan and Trengganu were separate protected States, commonly known as the Unfederated Malay States. Johore, which before had had a British consular agent, asked for a British General Adviser in 1914, while rights of suzerainty over the other four States had been transferred to [Great Britain] in 1909 by Siam in return for the surrender of extra-territorial rights and a loan for the construction of a railway through Siamese Malaya.

Between the Straits Settlements and the Malay States were certain political differences. The Crown Colony was British territory, so that a person born in the Straits Settlements was . . . a natural-born British subject eligible for a British passport. Under [the British] the Ruler of a Malay State remained juridically an independent sovereign, though he had surrendered his political independence by treaty, so that a person born in a Malay State was a British protected person and granted a certificate of nationality in lieu of passport. The difference of status between those born in the Colony and those born in the protectorate may seem the difference between Tweedledum and Tweedledee, but it would be one of the obstacles . . . to giving back Province Wellesley to Kedah and Malacca to Johore, in order to induce them to enter the Federation.

Unlike the ordinances of the Crown Colony, the enactments of the Malay States were not subject to the [Britannic] King's veto: they needed only the assent of the Malay Rulers. His [Britannic]

[1] See Selection 12.
[2] See Selection 1.

Majesty could legislate for the Colony by Orders in Council but not for any Malay State. In the Colony the King delegated the royal prerogative of mercy to the Governor; in a Malay State the review of death sentences lay with the Ruler in Council. In the Colony land was held from the Crown, in a Malay State from its Sultan. Unlike the annual estimates of the Colony, those of the Malay States did not require the sanction of the Secretary of State for the Colonies but were only forwarded for his information. In the Councils of the Colony the Governor presided; in every State Council the Ruler was President.

Broadly, Downing Street directed the administration of the Straits Settlements but advised the Governments of the various Malay States.

THE STRAITS SETTLEMENTS

The Governor of the Straits Settlements acted after 1867 under the authority of the Secretary of State for the Colonies, who is himself responsible to the British Parliament. Though he was titular Commander-in-Chief, in peace except for co-ordinating such civil matters as transport and supply with military measures for defence, the Governor was expected to play no part at all in military affairs, which were solely the concern of the Cabinet, the Committee for Imperial Defence, the Admiralty, the War Office and the Air Ministry; without the sanction of Downing Street or unless there arose urgent necessity, he could assent to no Bill "interfering with the discipline or control of His Majesty's forces"; even if the Governor recommended the formation of volunteer regiments, he might be overruled, and in time of war a real soldier might usurp any of his functions considered necessary for defence. The Governor had the advice of an Executive Council, which it was incumbent upon him to consult on all important matters not too urgent to be put before it "or of such a nature that reference to it would prejudice the public weal". This small Council comprised the General Officer Commanding the troops, leading civilian officials and three unofficials, of whom one was a Chinese and another had been a Eurasian.

The British Parliament is the final legislative, as also the final executive, authority for all Crown Colonies. But it legislates for them only on exceptional occasions, as when a law embodying their constitution is amended or Crown land like the Dindings is given back to a native ruler or there is need for some law on currency that is not appropriate for local legislation. For the rest, all legislation in Crown Colonies is local and passed by the local Legislative Council. In the Straits Settlements that Council in its latest shape was composed of the Governor as President, with thirteen official and thirteen unofficial members, all of whom had to be British subjects. Two of the unofficial members had since 1924 been chosen, one by the British members of the Singapore Chamber of Commerce and the other by those of the Penang Chamber. The rest, namely five Europeans, three Chinese, one British Indian and one Eurasian, were nominated by the Governor. The Governor had both an original and casting vote, so that there was an official majority. Without instructions from Downing Street or unless urgent necessity arose, the Governor could assent to no Bill subjecting persons not of European descent to disabilities or restrictions not shared by Europeans. The official majority was never used normally except on the instructions of the Secretary of State, and policy was greatly influenced by local public opinion and the local Press. Difficult issues were debated informally and settled as far as possible outside the Council chamber, as in practice they are even under a parliamentary government.

Two points are notable. Unofficial members were nominated and not elected, owing to the difficulty of compiling an electoral roll from a floating population of many races and the impracticability of distinguishing between British subjects and foreigners at a polling booth. Secondly, the need for an official majority on rare occasions arose from the fact that members were representatives not of a homogeneous community but of different races with interests bound occasionally to conflict. Most of the inhabitants of the Colony were foreigners content to live under an administration efficient, honest and impartial. Only a few Europeans and Straits-born Chinese inclined to democratic self-government, without weighing the composite character of the electorate and the difficulty of securing representation satisfactory to Malay, Chinese and Indian interests.

THE FEDERATED MALAY STATES

The gist of the treaties with these States was that all revenues should be collected and all appointments made in the name of each Ruler, and that each Ruler should receive a British Resident "whose advice must be asked and acted upon on all questions other than those touching Malay religion and customs".

But the four States came under British protection at various dates between 1874 and [1887] and were administered originally as separate entities. Each had a State Council, that joined the functions of the Executive and Legislative Councils of a Crown Colony. Each passed its own laws and its own annual budget and had its own State officers. In spite of the Residents being subordinate to the Governor of the Straits Settlements, lack of communications with Singapore soon led to serious divergencies in the laws, taxation and land administration of the different States.

Accordingly in 1895 the four States were federalized with one civil service, under a Resident-General subordinate to the Governor. The powers of the Malay Sultans were to remain uncurtailed, except that in all matters of administration other than those touching the Mohammedan religion they were to follow the advice of the new Resident-General, while the obligations of each to accept the advice of his Resident remained. The then Sultan of Perak observed that he had never heard of a ship with two captains, and the event was to show that the Governor in Singapore made a third. The absence of an Executive Council to advise and check him encouraged intolerance of restraint in the chief resident officer of the new federation, who quickly assumed complete executive control over the administration and sometimes opposed a Governor's policy. When the latter attempted in 1911 to stress the subordinate nature of the office of Resident-General by changing the title to Chief Secretary, this step only made Europeans, Chinese and Malays suspicious that it was desired to weaken the office and deprive the Malay States of a champion against encroachments by

Singapore and by Downing Street. And what is there in a name? Still uncontrolled by any Executive Council, the Chief Secretary at Kuala Lumpor waxed fat and might at any time kick against the pricks of Singapore.

In 1895 there had been instituted a purely advisory Federal Durbar with no legislative or financial power. In 1909, to safeguard the big tin and rubber industries, which covered all Malaya, Sir John Anderson, the first Governor to be styled High Commissioner for the Malay States, established a Federal Council which left to the four State Councils only the confirmation of death sentences, the banishment of alien criminals, the appointment of mosque and village officials, and occasional legislation on trifling points of Moslem law and native custom. The Rulers were for eighteen years members of the new Federal Council, but Their Highnesses had more dignity and sense than to bandy words with officials and Chinese merchants in open assembly. In 1895 the four Rulers had agreed to give to those States in the Federation which required it such assistance in money and officials as the British Government advised. From 1909 these same Rulers and their Residents (although previously consulted outside the council chamber) sat and listened to what seemed to the public the allocation of the revenue of their States by their Residents' official chief and by the unofficials whose main care was the tin and rubber industries. The amazing prosperity of those industries between 1909 and 1914 blinded the eyes of everyone to the creeping tentacles of bureaucracy. And then the emergencies of the [First] World War with the need for urgent and simultaneous legislation turned the federation into an amalgamation.

With the lean years of depression after the war, everywhere men took stock of their governments, not always fairly. In Malaya roads and railways and surveys overleaping State boundaries, uniform legislation, a uniform postal service, a civil service common to the whole peninsula, an Institute for Medical Research, the Sultan Idris College for the Malay teachers of the Federation and Colony, these and many other conveniences had in a few years come to be accepted as part of the nature of Malayan things and were hardly appreciated as the direct result of federation.

Instead critics complained that the Kuala Lumpor Juggernaut

had often blundered in its tracks. No doubt it was the fault of the experts, but still millions of dollars had been sunk in the drifting silt of the new dock constructed at Prai opposite Penang to serve the Federal railway. And then there was that railway, built, it is true, out of revenue, but therefore built extravagantly and planned for the future without thought of the rapid development of motor traffic. Moreover the Malay Sultans saw how it was the pooling of their revenues that had financed a loan to Siam after the Anglo-Siamese treaty of 1909 and so brought under British protection four new Malay States, each with a State Council such as their own States also had enjoyed constitutionally before the creation of the Federal Council. The Rulers of the Federated States were chagrined. "These last have continued one hour only, and thou hast made them" more than "the equal unto us, which have borne the burden and heat of the day". So in spite of Kuala Lumpor's nervousness at the weakening of central control, and its protests against the "fetters of Singapore," proposals were mooted that the Chief Secretary's powers should be distributed between Rulers, British Residents and Heads of Departments, and his place taken by a Federal Secretary junior to all the Residents. In 1935 this change, the key-stone to any policy of decentralization, was approved in Downing Street and carried out. Laws in future had to be passed not by the Federal Council but by the four State Councils. There was also a measure of financial devolution from the Federal Council to the several States.

To maintain the financial stability of the federation, control over the provision of many services was retained by its Council. These services comprised its public debt and the pensions of federal officers, unified services (like the customs, police, survey, labour, and military defence), federal officers and institutions. But instead of the Federal Council deciding the detailed expenditure of the agricultural, co-operative, educational, electrical, forest, medical, mining, prison and veterinary departments and the department of public works, it was to continue a recent practice of voting each State annually a block grant for these services within its own borders. Each State would have some freedom in allocating the money to the various departments, and it was anticipated that the State authorities being on the spot would be better able to check extravagance than the Federal heads in Kuala Lumpor. But the High Commissioner was to approve each Resident's estimates before they were submitted to his State Council and he could veto or direct expenditure on any specific object. Nor could any State raise a loan without the consent of the Federal Council. The financial stability of the Federated States remained secure.

The enlargement of each State's spending and legislative powers demanded more enlightened representation on the effete State Councils, following the lines on which the Federal Council had been reformed and strengthened while its existence was the subject of criticism. In 1927 the four Sultans to their great relief had vacated their seats in favour of four Malay unofficials free to speak their minds. In the following year an Indian member was added to the five European and two Chinese unofficials. And the officials included, not as originally a Resident-General and the four Residents only, but the Advisers on finance, education, medical services, agriculture, public works, and Chinese affairs, with the heads of the Customs and Labour Departments and the General Manager of the Railways. In spite of its official majority, the Federal Council was a virile body competent to represent and urge the views of all classes—except perhaps labour, which had only an official representative.

Was it possible to reform the State Councils, also, to make their members vocal representatives of the public instead of the yes-men of a bureaucratic administration, whose voice was the voice of the British Resident and whose hands were those of the Malay Ruler signing ever law and order laid before him? Hitherto the members of State Councils had been the Sultan, the Resident, the major Malay chiefs, perhaps a British unofficial and one or two Chinese unofficials, the last an alien element admitted on British advice. There were no Indian unofficials, and proceedings were conducted in Malay and not, as by the Federal Council, in English. No Malay member ever voted against his Ruler—except in Negri Sembilan, where the Ruler was in theory only an arbiter and in practice never asked to arbitrate; and the cleverest Malay member of a State Council was ordinarily one who could talk longest without expressing any conclusive views before he had learnt those of his Sultan. To reanimate this feudal body, Europeans, Chinese and

Indian unofficials and some Malays educated in English and on modern lines were added. And it was made a rule that all unofficials on the Federal Council would be appointed from among the members of the State Councils. The day of the Malay Polonius had passed. The Europeans, Chinese and Indians, at any rate, criticized and debated without fear or favour. All of the new members of the reformed State Councils enjoyed their platform except indeed the unfortunate Financial Adviser, who was a member of all State Councils as well as of the Federal. A fellow sufferer was the Legal Adviser, who instead of piloting a Bill once through the Federal Council had to pilot identical Bills through four State Councils, his business being to see that there was no tampering with the uniformity of legislation. Include the five Unfederated States (one with an area of only 316 square miles), and there were now nine sets of identical laws in States that combined are about the size of England! Prodigious! The pretence of State autonomy had become Gilbertian. "Sir," said Dr. Johnson upon one occasion, "most schemes of political improvement are very laughable things."

THE UNFEDERATED MALAY STATES

In spite of a diversity of language, the treaties with the Unfederated States all had the same purport as those with the Federated, namely, that each State should ask and act upon British advice in all matters not touching Malay religion and custom. Johore, with an eye on the nomenclature of independent Siam, preferred the title General Adviser, an anomalous style without significance. The Johore treaty stipulated that if the Sultan and General Adviser disagreed, the views of both should be referred to the High Commissioner, but that was a course which would have been followed in any Malay State. The Sultan of Johore reserved the right to appoint members to his Councils and to recommend the removal or dismissal of unacceptable officers seconded to his State, but those again were among the privileges of all Rulers. An important anomaly both in the Johore and in the Kedah treaties was the stipulation that in Kedah the official language, in the absence of special authority, was to be Malay and that in Johore Malay should rank with English as an official language. Both Johore and Kedah stipulated that Malays in the service should be treated on terms of equality with Europeans.

Unlike the other States Johore had a written constitution dating from 1895 with three advisory councils instead of the usual one State Council. There was a Council of Malay Ministers that met *in camera* and discussed domestic politics but had no powers executive or legal; there was a most useful Executive Council, that met every Sunday under the Sultan and debated and controlled the general executive business of the State, and there was a Council of State corresponding to the Legislative Council of the colony which had for its president the Malay Prime Minister. Both the Executive and Legislative Councils of Johore had European, Chinese and Indian members as well as Malay.

In spite of the essence of treaties with all the Malay States being identical, the position of an Adviser in an Unfederated Malay State was different from that of a Resident in a Federated. The Malays of Johore and Kedah were educated and sophisticated and had made some show of running their own government before [British] entry, so that it was fair and politic and natural to consult them and let them have a voice in administration. Again Kelantan and Trengganu had some educated chiefs, quite different from the Malay chiefs seventy years ago. They were also too poor and too remote to attract much foreign capital, had a large and predominantly Malay population, and had neither the need for many European officers nor the money to pay for them, so that there too the administration was mainly Malay and the British representative perforce an adviser.

None of these new States was prepared to enter the Federation or surrender one iota of its administrative independence to a Federal Council. Each passed its own laws, although copied from those of the Federation. No scheme of decentralization deceived them; the bait of a united Malaya was dangled before them in vain. Not till recently was it considered politic or quite delicate to ask them even to defray the emoluments of a federal officer lent to them for a lengthy tour of inspection. Indeed, only the more intrepid federal heads ever ventured to inspect the work of their subordinates in the Unfederated States, and then, as a cynic once remarked, their visits resembled those of Foreign Secretaries on placatory missions to Hitler or Mussolini in the days before the war. For such visits, it is true, the Unfederated States paid willingly, glad to see these gentlemen as their own temporary officers, but if they realized all the debt they had owed and still were owing to federal experts, federal laws, federal reputation in the world of international commerce, they kept mum, praying that the broom of interference might never destroy the cobwebs of isolation, to which they were so accustomed and so inclined. Being good Moslems, perhaps they reflected at times how on one occasion cobwebs across the mouth of a cave saved the life of their Prophet.

17. British Colonial Rule in Burma

The following selection is extracted from British Rule in Burma 1824-1942 *(Faber and Faber, London, 1946, pp. 77-86), by G. E. Harvey, who served for many years as a member of the Indian Civil Service and who therefore writes with the authority of direct experience of the British colonial regime in Burma. Reprinted by permission.*

Until 1862 Burma was governed by post from Calcutta: a daily post to Akyab was established immediately after the 1826 annexation, and local initiative was discouraged. In 1862 however Burma received a governor of her own at Rangoon (he was not actually styled governor till much later because the title was as sacrosanct in the Indian as it is common in the colonial empire).

Of the eighteen governors since 1862, the last two were from England, men with parliamentary experience. All the others were members of the Indian Civil Service, and only four of them had served in Burma, the rest being from India. Indeed as late as 1900 nearly a third of the service in Burma had spent the formative years of their career in India.

Laws were made in India till 1897 when the governor was given a legislative council; its numbers rose to thirty, half of them natives, but they were all nominated and there was a strong official bloc.

Not only were many of the laws now made in Burma, but administration was increasingly devolved, even though British-Indian principles still applied.

The country was everywhere in the hands of a bureaucracy. Only the highest ranks were English, and numerous intermediate posts provided the Burmese with a career, often in positions of considerable authority. But it kept them in a straight jacket as administrators; it provided no outlet for men who, though capable of leadership, were unable to pass examinations or unwilling to face the lifelong grind: it prevented the circulation of the red corpuscles in the blood of the body politic. And it gave the people no means of shaping the laws under which even administrators of their own race had to operate.

All this changed, and the change began with the creation of the first parliament in 1923.

DYARCHY 1923-37

The first parliamentary system, which lasted fourteen years, was real enough, freely elected, with ministers it could call to account even if they held only half the portfolios, and the less essential ones at that.

Law and order, irrigation, revenue and finance, the major bureaucracy in charge of general administration, were reserved to two members of the governor's council; one of them was always a Burman, and they both sat in parliament, but they were not elected and in the last resort they could claim privilege.

Local government, education, public health, agriculture, excise, public works and forests were transferred to two ministers, fully answerable to parliament and of course chosen from among its members. In the governor's study they sat at the table as of right alongside his two members of council, and thus three of the big five who ruled Burma were Burmese.

The issue never arose, because men were feeling their way, but the flaw in dyarchy is that finance in itself suffices to render government indivisible. Not only did the members of council in the last resort control the budget, they always had first claim on it for their own departments, and though they met the ministers half-way, the ministers knew it was no use asking for more. Thus—it is an imaginary case, but it concerns the nation-building departments of which they were in charge—if the ministers had wished to undertake large-scale reforms involving heavy expenditure on education and public health, they could never have done so, as they only controlled half the budget and had no power to rearrange the other half.

The reader may think the system was only a façade. But nobody who was there and witnessed the change, especially if he were on the inside of the machine, is likely to forget it. The year 1923 was the parting of the ways.

LOCAL GOVERNMENT

This was introduced in the districts, along with parliamentary government at the centre, in 1923. Municipalities were already in existence but hitherto they had always had the most senior civil servant in the neighbourhood, usually the deputy commissioner, as chairman; he was now eliminated. And district councils, corresponding to [British] county councils, were created for the first time; they were of course entirely elective.

Outside Rangoon there were only two dozen places in the whole country you could really call a town; yet there were no fewer than 58 municipalities. More than half had under 10,000 inhabitants and less than £7,000 income, even including central grants; outside a street or two facing the bazaar they were really villages. As long as the chairman was a civil servant there was at any rate a semblance of work. Its cessation, when he was eliminated, was no great loss, for it was only a semblance concealing the true state of affairs. In some places there was even an improvement, for here and there the ratepayers showed a willingness to tax themselves for the sake of a water supply or street lighting scheme. But usually there was a deterioration, for the electors were apathetic, the councillors unable to stand up to a corrupt chairman and the staff who shared his rake-off. In one town they could never be induced to have an infant welfare society or even a midwife though the infant mortality rate was 507 per mille, i.e. half the newborn babies died. And the greatest of all, Mandalay itself, with a population of 140,000 and a large enough staff to get a little work done if the council-lors wanted it, sometimes had to be suspended for two or three years at a time.

Similarly with the 28 district councils. Not that it was entirely their fault. In practice they were allowed so little power that they had no incentive. The taxation they levied was only about six-pence a head, as the central government had endowed them with sufficient sources of income to meet most of their modest obliga-tions. Some of them managed their roads, and even their schools, effectively enough, but in others the staff might remain unpaid for months because personal differences made it impossible to get a quorum, even for the purpose of electing a chairman.

It is not, as some people imagine, that Burmans are inherently corrupt or unable to run a show. The great pagoda festivals prove the contrary: the organization behind them may be informal but it gets there just the same, and with remarkably little corruption. But here the Burman has a tradition—he is interested in pagoda festi-vals.

The system of local government [the British] introduced was the result of a thousand years' experience in a totally different society. None of the classes which provide the real stiffening on local bodies in England had any counterpart in Burma, and the whole thing was an alien make-believe with its formal committee meet-ings, type-script agenda, resolutions, amendments and counter-amendments. As for the model bye-laws on which the central gov-ernment insisted, in the matter of sanitation for instance, they were perfectly admirable on paper but they often overlooked the primitive conditions obtaining in the locality.

Rangoon corporation was in a class by itself. A cosmopolitan seaport with half a million people it was open to inspection by the outer world, so that despite a great deal of graft it was moderately efficient and had good credit in the loan market. But it was running largely under the old momentum, and the staff it inherited from bureaucratic times was being replaced by men who had to pay heavily for their appointments. Moreover racial friction was increasing; although Indians constituted more than half the pop-ulation and paid 55 per cent of the taxes, the Burmese (who con-stituted less than a third of the population and paid only 11 per cent of the taxes) said it was the capital of their country, the corporation should be under their control, and the system whereby the different races held the mayoralty in rotation should cease.

SEPARATION FROM INDIA 1937

Burmans, as distinct from the other Burmese races, can claim to be a nation, a rare thing in India. The English firms at Rangoon declared for separation as early as 1884, if only out of local patriotism; but recently, when it came to the point, some of them hesitated, for the xenophobia of the Burman was now unconcealed.

Burmans themselves, even when inarticulate, always resented the connection. Just as when they had kings of their own they refused to receive an ambassador from the viceroy of India, insisting on one from the King of England himself, so now they desired to deal direct with the people of England, as nation with nation. There was also colour prejudice: they regard Indians as black men. Yet, underlying all this, is a true instinct: in his heart, the feeling the Burman has for English civilization at its best amounts almost to veneration, and he wishes to deal with the source direct.

The anti-separation majority at the 1932 election, fought on this issue, was merely a manœuvre. Burmans wanted to have it both ways, both to join and to leave the proposed Indian federation, to stay in until India got dominion status and then to walk out, taking dominion status with them. They knew that the Indian Congress Party set the pace, it was Congress who would get dominion status, and they feared that, once separated and left without Indian support, they would become a mere crown colony, a white man's preserve. In vain did the Ramsay MacDonald [United Kingdom Labor] government assure them that separation would not prejudice the future, that even if separated they would advance at the same rate as India, that self-government was the goal for all, that they were free to enter the federation or stay out, but the choice once made must be final. The Burma parliament would believe no assurances, they persisted in returning ambiguous answers, and finally the London government decided the only interpretation to be placed on these answers was that Burma desired separation. She got it in 1937 (simultaneously with the new constitution), and nothing more was heard of the anti-separation case, even from the most vociferous.

But it was unfortunate that separation synchronized with the new constitution, and that both were promised in a period of unemployment. The triple event was too much for the people.

They were a people who had only just imbibed the heady doctrine of self-determination. Actually it is an old and chastening doctrine but they understood it in a sense that would have surprised President Wilson: like all his precedessors in the long line of its exponents, he taught that it was only half the doctrine, the other half being self-restraint.

And though the world slump, which hit Burma in 1931, did not hit her as hard as some countries, the people had never known unemployment before. And as big business was all in foreign hands, they blamed it on the foreigner. From now on, year in, year out, the press and the platform told them they were the finest but most ill-used people in the world.

When the news of separation came through, it was hailed as more than mere separation from India: it was the beginning of national independence. The new constitution would bring it; many of the simpler-minded voters thought there'd be no taxes to pay under the new constitution, indeed the crops would grow of their own accord.

THE 1937 CONSTITUTION

The 1935 Government of India Act not only carried the Montagu-Chelmsford reforms a stage further, giving the provinces increased powers and providing for federation at the centre, it also separated Burma from India. And the new Burma constitution included the powers which in India went to the centre as well as those given to the provinces; hence the Burmese ministers had wider powers than the ministers of any Indian province.

Dyarchy was displaced by a complete cabinet, the single chamber by two, an upper (senate) and lower (representatives).

The senate had 36 members, half elected, the other half nominated (four were English, two of them elected); it could always be overridden by

The house of representatives, which had 132 seats, all elected. There were a few special constituencies for industrial labour (Burman and Indian), the various chambers of commerce (Burman, Chinese, Indian and English), and racial minorities (Karen, Indian and English) but 72 per cent of the seats were allotted to Burmans and it was they who dominated the house.

The cabinet, usually six to nine ministers, was appointed by the governor on the advice of the premier, the leader with the largest following in the house of representatives.

The governor had two counsellors and a financial adviser, high English officers whose advice was also available to the ministers, and they could address but were not members of either house; and in 1940, owing to the war, he appointed an additional counsellor, a Burman, to assist in defence.

The governor alone, and not parliament, was responsible for foreign affairs, defence, currency and the Excluded Areas. And he was also empowered to override parliament in matters gravely affecting the peace and tranquillity, the financial stability and credit of the country, the rights of minorities, certain backward areas, the services, racial and commercial discrimination. It is an imposing list, but more imposing on paper than in reality, as the sufferers . . . discovered to their cost. Many of the safeguards in the written constitution of Burma correspond to the unwritten conventions of the British constitution or to powers exercised under the prerogative. The difference lies not in the reservation of power but in the fact that with [the British] the executive are, however, indirectly, answerable; and they are men of [British] race. Even so, the Burmese cabinet had as much power in internal affairs as the cabinet of many a sovereign state.

The exclusion of the Excluded Areas—which meant that the ministers' writ did not run, and parliament had no say, in half of all that is shown as Burma on the map—was in no way anomalous. These areas are not, and never were, Burmese. They were not subject to the 1923 parliament, and even before, in the days of the old bureaucracy, they were the governor's personal concern in which his officers for Burma Proper had no say.

The ministers were entitled to joint consultations with the governor's representatives. Thus, the interests of Burma Proper and of the Excluded Areas may overlap; and when, after the outbreak of [the Second World] war, a defence council was constituted, ministers sat among the soldiers.

The proceedings of the senate often reached a responsible level. Even in the house of representatives . . . there was plain speaking, and the truth was already beginning to come out in a way that is possible only in a parliament. Free speech, with all its difficulties for an untried public, but also with its benefits, has come to stay; and when in due course Burma produces a masterful executive, of a type more familiar in the east than [in the United Kingdom], even he may find these two chambers, or something like them, of inestimable value.

THE FRANCHISE

The franchise could hardly have been wider. Men voted at 18 (against 21 in England), and women, subject to a literacy test, at 21 —there were three lady members of parliament. The electorate numbered nearly three million, 24 per cent of the gross population in the parliamentary area (against only 12 per cent in India); in England the figure is 71 per cent but fully half the adult population of a constituency in Burma may be illiterate, alien, or migratory. In keen constituencies two-thirds of the roll actually voted, a striking contrast to Siam where, after the franchise had been introduced in 1933 in response to an alleged popular demand, at most 9 per cent troubled to vote.

EXCLUDED AREAS

	square miles	per cent	million people	per cent
Parliamentary Burma	149,000	57	12.3	84
Excluded Areas	113,000	43	2.4	16
All Burma	262,000	100	15	100

When U Saw, the Burman premier, visited Mr. [Winston] Churchill in 1941 asking for dominion status, he gave the public the impression that he was speaking for all Burma. But . . . [none of the excluded areas] is under the premier, and the ministers have no juris-

diction there. The Burmese cabinet is only for Burma, and the
. . . [excluded areas] is not Burma: it was added by [the British],
after [the British] had overthrown the kingdom of Burma in
1885. . . .

[The excluded areas coincide] with the hills, the great arc of frontier hills guarding Burma, shutting her off from India, China and
northern Siam. With one solitary exception, the Burman never occupied those hills.

The exception is the Shan States. Most of the Shan states—not
all—were tributary to the king of Burma, but even when the tribute was more than nominal, it was paid to His Burman Majesty in
person, not to his ministers. The Shan chiefs were kings in subordinate alliance with their overlord the king of Burma, and they
were not subordinate to his ministers.

As for the other areas, the Burman knew nothing of them beyond the valleys through which he marched in the course of his
campaigns, his invasions of Assam. He never knew the hills, indeed there are no less than 1,300 miles of Assam and Yunnan
frontier he never saw. [The British] had to explore those hills with
Indian surveyors, escorted by Indian troops, and often the people
only accepted [the British] on the condition, express or implied,
that [the British] ruled them [themselves]. Some of them had never
met the Burman; others had bitter memories of him.

Most of the people are illiterate save here and there among the
Shans, for the Shans have a Buddhist culture of the same fine medieval type as the Burmese themselves; it came from the same
source, along the caravan routes from northern India, indeed after
the middle ages it came from Burma itself, for the Burmese court
was a cultural centre.

It was Buddhism that brought writing to the Shans, and it did
not penetrate the other areas. The tribes there are illiterate pagans,
and their beliefs require the Wa to be headhunters, the Naga to
offer similar forms of human sacrifice, but this does not happen in
administered territory, and most of the other tribes are decent
enough, some of them perfectly charming.

There are literally scores of different tribes each with its own
language and distinctive costume, and very proud of it they are
too. Some of them, though broken up into clans, are quite numer-

ous, the Chin numbering 350,000, the Kachin 160,000, and it is these that form the backbone of the regiments. . . . The tribes are ruled by their chieftains or councils of tribal elders, for there is little uniformity. They have English officers to look after them, but only a few, with semi-political functions; thus, there are only five in the Chin hills, an area larger than Wales.

Similarly in the Federated Shan States, as large as England and Wales, there are only fourteen. The three dozen Shan states are miniature monarchies, each with its little court, most of them tiny, indeed rural, others the size of Devon and Cornwall combined, the size of a kingdom in Saxon England. You may think it extravagant to have so many courts for 1½ million people, but that is because you do not know what they are. The privy purse of some Shan chiefs is only a few hundred a year; the richest has £5,000, with many charitable calls to meet. The palace is smaller than many a modest country house in England, indeed it is often rustic, built of thatch. Yet the little throne is revered by the people, it means much to them, it has a history behind it, and more often than you would imagine, its occupant is beloved.

It is a false outlook that regards these areas as inferior and their political development as merely retarded. The Montenegrin mountaineer is unable to read or write but he isn't retarded, he's a freer man than the shop assistant in Cellophaneville the dormitory suburb. When General [Ord] Wingate trained the 1943 commando raid into Burma, he trained it in these areas, with some of these very people, and . . . he said—that his savages often showed an initiative and intelligence that put their civilized comrades to shame.

18. French Rule in Cambodia

Unlike the earlier selections in this chapter, the following account of French rule in Cambodia has been written by an American scholar, Martin F. Herz, who has had no direct association with the colonial regime. It presents within short compass a critical account of French rule and is extracted from A Short History of Cambodia from the Days of Angkor to the Present (*F. A. Praeger, New York, 1958, pp. 57-72*). *Reprinted by permission.*

King Ang Duong did not, of course, have in mind the kind of protectorate that was later imposed upon Cambodia. He had in mind a French guarantee of his country's independence in return for certain trade concessions. He sent a minister to Singapore to suggest such a treaty to the French consul there, but when the latter finally sent an emissary to Cambodia, the King of Siam heard about that mission and threatened Ang Duong with war if he signed any treaty with France. The Siamese overlordship would thus probably have continued if the French had not in 1859 defeated the Annamites and occupied Cochinchina, the part of Viet Nam that borders on Cambodia to the southeast. Ang Duong did not live to see the protectorate. He died in the same year and was succeeded by his son Norodom, but before the latter could be crowned a revolt broke out and he was forced to flee, first to Siamese-held Battambang and then to Bangkok, where he arrived with the royal insignia—the crown, sacred sword, and seal. In 1862, Norodom returned to Cambodia accompanied by Siamese troops, regained Udong, and installed himself there as King, although the Siamese prudently refused to send him his regalia until the situation had become stabilized.

King Norodom's position was thus weak, and it was rendered still weaker by the fact that France harbored in Saigon Prince Sivotha, the pretender to the Cambodian crown who had conducted the revolt of 1860. Moreover, France could claim co-suzerainty over Cambodia as successor to Annam. Various French representatives made this point in more or less friendly fashion, pointing to the protection they could offer against Siam. Finally, in 1863, a concrete proposition was put to the King by a special French emissary from Saigon, the now-famous Commander Doudart de Lagree: the Emperor of France offered to "transform" into a protectorate the rights of suzerainty over Cambodia which he possessed as successor of the Emperor of Annam. A French resident would be assigned to the King of Cambodia, and Cambodia would agree to receive no consuls of other countries without the approval of France. French citizens would have the right to establish themselves freely in Cambodia, and reciprocal rights were granted to Cambodians who might wish to establish themselves elsewhere in the French empire. In return, France would not only guarantee to protect Cambodia against external attack but would undertake also to "maintain order and peace in the kingdom"—which also meant that it would wash its hands of Prince Sivotha, the rival of Norodom. The draft treaty also provided for free entry of French goods and for extraterritorial courts to judge disputes between Frenchmen, whereas mixed courts would judge litigation between Frenchmen and Cambodians.

Faced with the choice of national extinction at the hands of the Siamese and this kind of protection offered by the French, Norodom signed; but the treaty first had to be sent to Paris for ratification by Emperor Napoleon III. In the meantime Siamese diplomacy applied severe pressure on Cambodia. The King of Siam not only threatened war but also called attention to the fact that he could withold indefinitely the royal insignia which were still in Bangkok. Faced with these threats, Norodom signed a secret treaty with Siam recognizing the latter's suzerainty over Cambodia and ceding definitely the provinces which were under Siamese occupation. But as soon as the approved treaty returned from Paris, the French in turn applied pressure on Siam and finally obtained the dispatch of the royal insignia. King Norodom was thus crowned in 1864 with the crown that had been obtained for him by the French and that was in fact handed to him at the ceremony by the new French resident. Siam could still nominally claim suzerainty and was represented at the coronation by an ambassador, but he was prevailed upon to leave after the ceremony. French hegemony over Cambodia can thus be said to date from the crowning of King Norodom.

King Norodom was not initially a French puppet, but he eventually became one. The French protectorate established under his rule was not uncontested by the Cambodian people. Revolts broke out from 1866 to 1867 and again from 1885 to 1887, but they were finally put down by French troops in support of the Cambodian army, which at that time was led by the King's brother, Prince Sisowath. The country was divided. Action against the French implied disloyalty to the King, who was the symbol of the country's very existence. The French were hated, but as long as the royal court supported them, they could control the country with relative ease.

After the first insurrection was beaten down, the French moved to regularize relations with Siam which, naturally, had supported the rebels. They negotiated a treaty by which the King of Siam was made to renounce "for himself and his successors any tribute, present, or other sign of vassalage on the part of the King of Cambodia." In return, the Emperor of France promised not to incorporate Cambodia into Cochinchina, which had meanwhile become a French colony, and recognised the definite possession by Siam of the provinces of Siemreap, Battambang, and Sisophon. This did not prevent France, however, from later negotiating new treaties by which those provinces were returned to Cambodia.

The protectorate became a virtual French colony in 1884 when King Norodom was forced to sign another document by which France assumed also control of the internal Cambodian administration. Under that treaty, the King undertook to "enact all the administrative, judicial, financial, and commercial reforms which the French government judges necessary in the interest of the protectorate." As a result, the entire Cambodian civil service was placed under the control of the resident. Frenchmen headed up the customs, internal revenue, postal, agricultural, forestry, health, veterinary, and other services, as well as the country's educational system. Residents and deputy residents were established in all the provincial capitals and other population centers, with all local Cambodian officials responsible to them through a Cambodian "mandarin" who was only nominally in charge. French troops were already established in the country, and to them was now added French control of the police. What distinguished the protectorate from a colony was essentially the institution of the royalty, which was still nominally the highest authority in the land. The French resident was an "advisor" to the King, but he had to have immediate access to the monarch, and the latter was obliged to accept his advice.

The overall record of the French protectorate, which lasted for almost ninety years, is difficult to assess, for there were many positive as well as negative aspects and these may well be given different weight by different observers. To allow the reader to form his own judgment, the accomplishments and liabilities of the protectorate will be enumerated below.

On the positive side, there can be no doubt, that the protectorate kept Cambodia in being as a nation. Had it not been for French protection, the country would eventually have been swallowed up by Siam—indeed, had it not been for the French occupation of Cochinchina, Cambodia might have been earlier swallowed up by Annam or divided between the latter and Siam. As a second positive point, one must list the recovery of the lost provinces. As mentioned above, the French recognition of Siamese conquest in the treaty of 1867 did not prevent France later from exerting armed pressure on Siam to disgorge various border regions. By a treaty in 1904 and another one in 1907, France won back the provinces of Battambang, Sisophon, and Siemreap as well as certain territories in northeastern Cambodia that had been occupied by the Siamese, all of which were reincorporated into Cambodia. Had it not been for the French, the great rice-growing area of western Cambodia, including the very ruins of Angkor, would today be located in an out-lying province of Thailand. Further on the positive side, one must mention the remarkable work done by French science in exploring and recovering the past glory of Cambodia through the reconstruction and interpretation of the monuments of Angkor. Cambodia owes the awareness of its own historic grandeur to the French protecting power.

The French also deserve credit for their policy of exalting the monarchical institution, which today represents a key factor of national unity and stability. To be sure, French rule exploited the loyalty which Cambodians owed their King—indeed, as long as the people owed allegiance to the monarch and the latter was controlled by the French, the country would be governed with an economy of means—but in assessing the positive and negative aspects of French rule no distinction should be made between intentional and unintentional benefits or shortcomings. As it is, it must be set down as a remarkable accomplishment that the Kings of Cambodia, due to French policy managed to retain their prestige and the allegiance of their subjects. The pomp and panoply surrounding the monarch were carefully maintained and respected. When the capital was moved from Udong to Phnom Penh in 1867, the King for a time lived in a palace that compared rather unfavorably with the French residence, but this was later corrected: the beautiful, authentically Cambodian royal palace which one may today admire, in Phnom Penh, with its sweeping lines, its stacked gables, traditional ornaments, and profuse wall decorations, was designed by a French architect and constructed by the French in 1915.

A device by which the royal family was effectively enfeebled, even while outwardly unaffected in its prestige, was the manner in which the protecting power influenced the succession: instead of bestowing the crown upon one of King Norodom's sons, the French resident proposed to the Crown Council that the succession should go to the deceased King's brother Sisowath, who had been so helpful to the French in beating down the two rebellions. Sisowath reigned from 1904 to 1927, and his loyalty to France was such that Cambodians actually fought in the French army in Europe during World War I. (Khim Tit, who in 1956 was prime minister of Cambodia, had been a corporal in the French Army in 1918.) King Monivong, who succeeded Sisowath, was the latter's son, and his accession to the throne thus consecrated the existence of two rival royal lines, that of Norodom and that of Sisowath.

The kings led an easy existence devoted to art and to what, to Western eyes, seems like debauchery but was in actual fact the expected conduct of Cambodian royalty. King Norodom still had some 200 wives, not counting concubines. The Sisowath branch was less wealthy (since Norodom passed his wealth to his children), thus more dependent on the French, but still able to maintain a sumptuous household. King Monivong still had some fifty wives, also not counting concubines. It was regarded as a signal honor to become a member of the royal ballet, and in Monivong's day all of those dancers were royal consorts.

After the death of King Monivong in 1941, the French were confronted with a difficult decision. The King's eldest son, Prince Monireth, appeared too independent-minded (and, indeed, independence-minded), so the French resident exerted his decisive influence on behalf of a younger member of the royal family who had the incidental merit of descending from both branches— Prince Sihanouk's father being a Norodom and his mother a Sisowath. Sihanouk seemed to the French to be more pliable, weak-willed, and accommodating. As is well known, they were mistaken in that appraisal.

Among the positive aspects of the French protectorate one may also mention the abolition of slavery, the strict division between executive and judiciary (the legislature was "consultative" and of no consequence), and the institution of an impartial system of justice which is still fondly and nostalgically remembered by Cambodians today. The civil administration was improved through the strengthening of the system of village headmen (Mekhums) who were given wide authority. A few hospitals were established. A fairly good road system was constructed. A railway was built from Phnom Penh to Battambang and thence to the Thai frontier. A small river port was constructed at Phnom Penh. City planning, both in the capital and in the provinces, deserves to be mentioned among the assets.

Economically, the country was not much developed except for the creation of rubber plantations, which were in effect French enclaves with foreign labor, contributing nothing to the economy but not draining out its substance. If economic development was scant, neither was there the rapacious type of colonialism found, for instance, in Dutch Indonesia.[1] Cambodia under the French was a backwater, a rear area, a stepchild. Most of the French failures came from neglect rather than from exploitation.

The greatest French sin of omission concerned the field of education. An educated Cambodian elite might have aspired to high posts in the country's administration, but the kind of education that was provided stopped well short of preparation for university study. A senior high school was provided only in 1935, and the number of graduates from that institution ("bacheliers") in 1939 was exactly four. There was, of course, no institution of higher learning in Cambodia, and Cambodians were discouraged from attending such institutions in France. Only one Cambodian obtained a medical doctor's degree in France before the war, and he was able to do so because he remained in France after enlisting in its army during World War I. Cambodia's only pre-war graduate en-

---

[1] See Selections 10 and 11.

gineer, Sonn Voeunsai (at present in charge of the national railways), is the son of that doctor who, having resided in France, was
able to overcome the obstacles in sending him there. Not a single
Cambodian could study architecture, nor were any trained to qualify for leading positions in the various government departments
such as agriculture, the postal service, public works, etc. By an ac-
cident Cambodia had one man (Sonn Sann) whose family had been
able to have him study at the École des Hautes Études Commer-
ciales in Paris and who thus had some qualifications to head the
new National Bank when it was created in 1954. The dearth of
trained executive talent is apalling.

University training of a sort was provided at the Indochinese
University at Hanoi toward the very end of the protectorate, but no
doctors were graduated there—only "medicins," and their number
was less than thirty in the case of Cambodians, proportionately
much less than the number of Vietnamese. In the case of teachers,
the record is even worse. Only three Cambodians were trained in
pedagogy at Hanoi and not a single one in France. Since there were
no Cambodians trained to teach high school, almost all the teachers
were provided by France, and to this day Cambodia is dependent
upon French teachers for most of the high school training it provides. The bulk of primary education was left to the Buddhist
pagodas. State-run primary schools numbered 107 (today there are
900) and, strangely enough, required the moppets to study French
from the very first year. But the pyramid of education quickly became needle-shaped.

A few figures show the contrast between the regime under the
French and under the present regime. In 1938 there were some 13,-
300 pupils in state elementary schools; in 1955/56 there were 195,-
100. On the next level ("école complementaire") the comparative
figures are 3,200 and 57,100. In 1938/39 only 238 Cambodian elementary school teachers were graduated; in 1955/56 the figure was
7,146, not counting an additional 1,060 teachers trained in special
accelerated courses which still could not meet the demand. Before
the war, France devoted less than 8 per cent of its Cambodian
budget to education. Today, the proportion is over 20 per cent, not
counting foreign aid. Despite the enormous effort undertaken today,
it will probably be a generation before Cambodia is able to obtain

the necessary numbers of much-needed specialists in the many fields required to run all government departments effectively.

For the sake of fairness, the French counter-argument to this record should also be stated. It is that Cambodians showed little interest in higher education during the protectorate, that pupils displayed a preference for the traditional pagoda schools over the new elementary schools that much effort was required to make them attend the latter and that, in short, the supply of education seemed to meet the demand. In the case of doctors, also, it is stated that the number of dispensaries set up by the French seemed entirely adequate in view of the reluctance of Cambodians to be treated by European methods.

Most of these arguments are correct as far as they go, but if there was little pressure for higher education it was because young Cambodians knew that there would be no careers for them in their own country; if pupils stayed away from the French-run elementary schools it was because they were French-run; if high school students did not attempt to pursue their studies it was because graduation was made exceedingly difficult for them; if European-trained doctors were not sought after by the population it was because no effort was made to acquaint the people with the benefits of European medicine.

Even today the curriculum of the Cambodian high schools, with its emphasis on French history and the teaching of all subjects (except Cambodian) in an alien language, represents a strange phenomenon. However, it must also be stated that if the grade-school moppets soon forgot the little French they had learned in their first three years, (which usually provided their entire schooling), thousands of other Cambodians have, thanks to their knowledge of French, had at least the possibility of communication with the outside world—when that communication became possible at the end of the protectorate.

It must be remembered that under the French regime there existed an entity called "Indochina," an artificial creation embodying today's Viet Nam (Tonkin, Annam and Cochinchina), Cambodia and Laos—an utterly anomalous entity that owed its existence only to French fiat and which has disappeared without a trace. The capitals of Indochina were Hanoi and Saigon, and it was normal—if one can speak of normalcy in the case of such an unnatural conglomeration—that customs, currency, and cultural and administrative services were concentrated in larger Vietnamese cities near the coast. This had a nefarious effect upon Cambodia: revenue from Cambodia was siphoned off for support of the services in Viet Nam; customs and currency offices were non-existent in Cambodia; all trade was transshipped at Saigon and usually financed and controlled from there. What is worse, since trained Vietnamese officials in the offices in Hanoi and Saigon were familiar with the overall administration of Indochina, it was natural that the French in Cambodia preferred to bring their Vietnamese assistants with them rather than train the under-educated Cambodians for such tasks.

The result was to intensify the inferiority of the Cambodians, and to make for an influx of foreigners across the nominal border separating Cambodia from Viet Nam. Today the French-imported Vietnamese administrators have departed from Cambodia, but there have been left behind some 300,000 other Vietnamese immigrants as well as some 250,000 Chinese who were brought or allowed in by the French. In the case of the Chinese in particular, their establishment in Cambodia has resulted in almost all business activity being held in their hands. Desperate and only partly successful attempts are being made today by the Cambodian government to rectify that situation and to place at least part of the economic power into the hands of Cambodians.

There is involved here, as a matter of fact, a strange liability which arose from the relatively egalitarian character of Cambodian society. There never were large landowners in Cambodia. The society was a simply one, with the King originally owning all land, and with only a small class of "mandarins" or court dignitaries who could pretend to any status of wealth. This idyllic situation militated against Cambodia: whereas in Viet Nam there were wealthy merchants or estate owners who sent their sons to study in France and who gradually inserted themselves into the productive and administrative processes, in Cambodia there was little native wealth available for investment or capable of exerting socio-political

influence. The most wealthy, enterprising, and gifted elements today are the Chinese, who now have a strangle-hold on import trade,
banking, rice-milling, money-lending, bus transportation, and the
distribution of almost all goods. This is a legacy of the protectorate
that is full of perilous foreboding for the future of Cambodia.

19. American Rule in the Philippines

*Following the national revolution against Spain (1896 to 1898),
the short-lived First Philippine Republic was established at Malolos
between January, 1899, and March, 1901. By the Treaty of Paris
(December, 1898), Spain had ceded the Philippines to the United
States and, after an initial period of indecision, President McKinley
declared that America would retain the Philippines, substituting
for the arbitrary rule of Spain "the mild sway of justice and right."
The next selection, extracted from* Philippine Political and Cultural History *(Philippine Education Company, Manila, 1957, II,
pp. 229, 247-257), by Gregorio F. Zaide, discusses from a Filipino
point of view certain aspects of American colonial policy in the
Philippines during the first three decades of the twentieth century.
The selection is reprinted by permission.*

The policy of the United States towards the Philippines was not
one of exploitation nor of permanent subjection, but rather a training in self-government and a preparation for ultimate independence. In his message to Congress in 1899, President William Mc-
Kinley said: "The Philippines are ours, not to exploit, but to
develop, to civilize, to educate, to train in the science of self-government."

Dr. Jacob G. Schurman, President of the First Philippine Commission, interpreted the American policy to mean "ever increasing
liberty and self-government . . . and it is the nature of such con-
tinuously expanding liberty to issue in independence."

All American Presidents, from McKinley to F. D. Roosevelt, and
all American Governors-General, from Taft to Murphy, declared

in their official statements that independence would someday be granted to the Philippines. The same policy was adopted by the Congress of the United States from 1899 to 1934. Both major political parties in America—the Republican Party and the Democratic Party—favored Philippine independence, with the only difference that the former would grant it after a long preparation on the part of the Filipino people for self-government, while the latter was willing to give it immediately. In 1908, for instance, the Republican Party platform advocated the policy of "leading the inhabitants step by step to an ever-increasing measure of home rule," while the Democratic Party platform favored "an immediate declaration of the nation's purpose to recognize the independence of the Philippine Islands." . . .

The triumph of the Democratic Party in the United States presidential election of 1912 was hailed with great joy by the Filipinos, for it meant the dawn of a new era in Philippine-American relations. In fact with President Wilson in the White House and Governor-General Francis Burton Harrison in Malacañan Palace, the Filipinos enjoyed the greatest measure of self-government hitherto denied to them. Harrison . . . allowed the Filipino officials to manage their own affairs. The next governor-general, Leonard Wood (1921-27), reversed the Harrisonian policy and came to blows with the Filipino officials. Fortunately his successors, Stimson, Davis, Roosevelt, Jr., and Murphy were men of liberal views; so the Filipino people were enabled to resume their march along the road of political democracy. The period from 1913 to 1935 was marked by progress in self-government—a fitting prelude to the rise of the Philippine Commonwealth. . . .

On October 6, 1913, Governor Francis Burton Harrison, former Democratic congressman for New York, arrived in Manila. In the colorful inaugural ceremonies, held . . . on that day, he delivered President Wilson's message to the Filipino people, as follows:

"We regard ourselves as trustees acting not for the advantage of the United States but for the benefit of the people of the Philippine Islands.

Every step we take will be taken with a view to the ultimate independence of the Islands and as a preparation for that independence. And we hope to move towards that end as rapidly as the safety and the permanent interests of the Islands will permit. After each step taken, experience will guide us to the next."

On his own part, Governor-General Harrison promised the jubilant Filipinos that he would give them all opportunities to exercise self-government. "People of the Philippine Islands!" he said, "A new era is dawning! We place within your reach the instruments of your redemption. The door of opportunity stands open and, under Divine Providence, the event is in your own hands." . . .

Shortly after Harrison's inauguration, President Wilson gave five out of nine seats in the Philippine Commission to the Filipinos. This meant the Filipino majority in the upper house of the legislature, and, since the Philippines Assembly (lower house) was composed of all Filipinos, this really gave them control of the legislative body. . . .

An outstanding feature of the new regime was the Filipinization of the government service. Governor Harrison, believing in giving the Filipinos the largest measure of autonomy by way of preparing them for independent nationhood, appointed them to various offices in the government. American office-holders were induced to retire under the Osmeña Retirement Act which was passed by the Philippine Legislature in 1916.

In 1913 there were 2,636 Americans and 6,363 Filipinos in the civil service. By 1921 the number of American employees and officials decreased to 614, while that of the Filipinos increased to 13,240. Governor Harrison consistently pursued his policy of Filipinization and won the affection and respect of the Filipino people. American job-seekers, who believed in the ignoble doctrine of colonial exploitation, naturally assailed Harrison's policy. They failed to realize that Harrison was merely putting into practice Taft's dictum of "The Philippines for the Filipinos." . . .

As early as March, 1912, Representative William Atkinson Jones, Virginia Democrat, introduced in Congress the first of the Philippine independence bills which bore his name. This bill, providing for complete independence in eight years, or in 1921, did not pass in the House of Representatives.

In July, 1914, he introduced another bill without a definite date of independence, and expressing in its preamble America's promise to grant independence "as soon as a stable government can be established" in the Philippines. With the strong support of Resident Commissioner [Manuel Luis] Quezon, a dashing crusader of freedom, the bill passed the House on October 14, 1914 by a vote of 211 to 59, but it was not acted upon by the Senate because of the opposition of many Republican senators.

At the opening of the next Congress, the debates on the Jones Bill of 1914 continued with unabated interest. This time the Senate was more radical than the House. Senator Clarke of Arkansas introduced an amendment granting independence to the Filipinos at the end of not less than two years and not more than four years from the date of approval of the act. The vote in the Senate on this amendment was a tie—41 to 41. The President of the Senate, Vice-President Marshall, cast the deciding vote in its favor. The Republicans and the Democrat-Catholic bloc in the House rejected the Clarke Amendment. After weeks of stormy sessions, both House and Senate finally agreed on the Jones Bill without the Clarke Amendment, and President Wilson signed it on August 26, 1916. . . .

The Jones Law of 1916, otherwise called Philippine Autonomy Act, stated in the preamble that "it was never the intention of the people of the United States in the incipiency of the war with Spain to make it a war of conquest or for territorial aggrandizement" and that "the purpose of the people of the United States is to withdraw their sovereignty over the Philippine Islands and to recognize their independence as soon as a stable government can be established therein."

The Law was virtually an American-made constitution providing for a complete form of autonomous government in the Philippines. In harmony with the Montesquiean doctrine of separation of powers, it demarcated governmental functions into executive, legislative, and judicial. The executive power was vested in an American Governor-General who was appointed by the President of the United States with the consent of the American Senate. He was assisted by a Cabinet consisting of all secretaries of departments, one of whom was the American Secretary of Public Instruction, who also served as Vice-Governor. The legislative power resided in an elective bicameral legislature. The upper house, called Senate, replacing the appointive Philippine Commission, was composed of 24 senators—22 elected by the people and 2 appointed by the governor-general to represent the non-Christian Filipinos. The lower house, called House of Representatives, was composed of 93 representatives —84 elected by the people and 9 appointed by the governor-general to represent the non-Christian Filipinos. The judicial power was exercised by the Supreme Court, the Courts of First Instance, and the Justice of the Peace Courts. The Chief Justice (Filipino) and Associate Justices (Filipinos and Americans) were appointed by the President with the consent of the American Senate.

The Jones Law contained a Bill of Rights; it defined Filipino citizenship; it continued the representation of the Philippines by two resident commissioners in Congress; it provided for a sound budgetary system; and it granted great powers to the new government, such as the control of public domain, the right to enact tariff laws (except those referring to American-Philippine trade), the power to organize the executive departments, and the control over domestic affairs. Certain restrictions were, however, imposed, notably: (1) veto power of the American President and the governor-general over the acts of the legislature; (2) approval of changes in coinage and currency laws by the President; (3) congressional regulation of trade between America and the Philippines; and (4) appeal of certain cases tried by the Philippine Supreme Court to the United States Supreme Court. . . .

The new legislature under the Jones Law was inaugurated at Manila on October 16, 1916. The Honorable Manuel L. Quezon, who had just returned from his brilliant work in America as resident commissioner, was chosen President of the Senate. The Honorable Sergio Osmeña, President of the Nacionalista Party, was elected Speaker of the House of Representatives. He had previously rejected Quezon's advice to run for the Senate because he believed that the No. 1 Filipino leader should be the Speaker of the House.

The *Nacionalistas* again dominated the legislature, having swept the elections of 1916 for both houses. They won practically all seats, except one in the Senate and seven in the House which were copped by the decadent *Progresista Party,* which fused with the

Democrata Party in 1917 to form the *Partido Democrata* (Democratic Party). . . .

The first Cabinet was organized by Governor-General Harrison on January 11, 1917. . . .

Speaker Osmeña was asked by his friends and colleagues in December, 1916, to assume the portfolio of the Department of the Interior so that he, as the leader of the Filipino people, could exert some influence in shaping national policies. He thumbed down the request in a long memorandum of January 3, 1917, stating his belief that he could wield the leadership of his party and people better as Speaker of the House of Representatives. Consequently, Senator Rafael Palma was named Secretary of the Interior. . . .

In order to secure cooperation and harmony between the executive department and the legislature, Governor-General Harrison created the Council of State by Executive Order No. 37, dated October 16, 1918. This body was composed of the Secretaries of Departments and the Senate President and the House Speaker. Its functions were to advise the governor-general on important matters, to prepare and approve the budget before the governor-general sent it to the legislature, and to determine the policies of the different executive departments. In addition to these functions, the Council of State exercised certain executive authority. For instance, in 1919, it drafted regulations penalizing the monopoly and speculation in rice; in 1920 it approved the action of the Secretary of Finance authorizing the Philippine National Bank to issue temporary notes; and in 1921 it authorized service contracts for American teachers for a period of not more than two years.

The President of the Council of State was Governor-General Harrison and the Vice-President was Speaker Osmeña. The council met once a week to discuss important matters of state. . . .

Governor-General Harrison embarked the government in business for the purpose of accelerating the economic development of the Philippines. This step was said to be unprecedented in American colonial administration and contrary to American political practices. The Philippine National Bank was established by the government in 1916 and it gave extensive loans to the sugar planters. The Manila Railroad Company and the Manila Hotel were purchased; the National Development Company, the National Coal Company, and the National Cement Company were created. The National Petroleum Company and the National Iron Company were authorized by the legislature, but not organized. . . .

Governor-General Harrison holds the record of the longest tenure among the American governors-general of the Philippines, having occupied the gubernatorial chair for eight years (1913-21). He interpreted the Jones Law most liberally, giving the Filipinos the greatest measure of self-government. . . .

In the presidential election of 1920 the Republican Party returned to power, and Warren G. Harding became the President. Governor Harrison resigned and left Manila on March 5, 1921. Vice-Governor Charles E. Yeater acted as Chief Executive until October 5, 1921, when General Leonard Wood assumed office. The Filipino people and their leaders received the new governor-general with misgivings, for he was known to be opposed to the independence aspiration of the Filipinos. He was the antithesis of the highly popular Harrison in personal qualities and political credo.

Governor Wood was an able, honest, and efficient administrator; but he was woefully lacking in personal charm, tact and diplomacy. Immediately upon assuming office, he pugnaciously declared his policy of enforcing the Jones Law to the very letter. In the first year of his term, he vetoed 16 bills passed by the Philippine Legislature. Senate President Quezon, Senator Osmeña, and other Filipino leaders were alarmed and chagrined at his indiscriminate exercise of the veto power. It should be noted that Harrison throughout his whole term of office (1913-21), vetoed only five bills.

The tensed relations between Governor Wood and the Filipino leaders exploded in the dramatic "Cabinet Crisis of 1923". This was caused by the "Conley Affair". Mr. Ray Conley, an American detective in the police force of Manila, was suspended by Dr. Jose P. Laurel, Secretary of the Interior, because of the administrative charges filed against him. Governor Wood intervened and ordered Secretary Laurel to reinstate Conley. Out of deference to his superior's command, Dr. Laurel obeyed and then resigned. Because of the high-handed action of Governor Wood which was believed to be a curtailment of self-government, all the Filipino members of the Cabinet and the Council of State resigned on July 17, 1923.

Governor Wood accepted the resignations and continued to conduct the affairs of the government with the aid of his army advisers, who were dubbed "Cavalry Cabinet" by newspapermen. The Filipino leaders appealed to Washington, requesting the recall of the unpopular governor-general. But President Coolidge supported Wood, and, instead, rebuked them for their non-cooperation stand.

On November 9, 1926, Governor Wood abolished the Board of Control on the ground that it was unconstitutional since it assumed the powers that belonged only to the Chief Executive. This aroused another storm of indignation throughout the land. The Philippine Supreme Court sustained Wood, and its decision on the case was confirmed by the Supreme Court of the United States. Again Senate President Quezon, Senator Osmeña, and House Speaker Manuel Roxas were defeated, but they did not give up their political fight for self-government. . . .

On August 7, 1927, General Wood, who was vacationing in the United States, died, and with him passed the greatest long-drawn-out fight in the constitutional annals of the Philippines. Despite his wranglings with the Filipino leaders and notwithstanding his unpopularity with the people, his administration was productive of beneficent results. Honest and efficient, he swept away all [graft] and nepotism in the government offices. He stabilized the government finance, improved public sanitation and health, and developed the facilities of communication and transportation. Because of his notable contribution to the care of the lepers, the Leonard Wood Memorial Fund (otherwise called American Leper Association) was established after his death. . . .

Three Republican governors-general followed General Wood, as follows: Henry L. Stimson (1928-29), Dwight F. Davis (1929-32), and Theodore Roosevelt Jr. (1932-33). In their administration, they pursued a policy "between the liberalism of Harrison and the conservation of Wood", and thus restored the harmonious relations between the Malacañan Palace and the Philippine Legislature. . . .

With the victory of the Democratic Party in the presidential election of 1932, the Filipinos expected a better deal from America. True to their expectation, President Franklin Delano Roosevelt gave them a magnanimous governor-general—the Honorable Frank

Murphy, the crusading Mayor of Detroit. In his impressive inaugural ceremonies at Manila, June 15, 1933, the new governor-general frankly told the Filipinos that he would devote his energies to the assurance of "peace and contentment of the people" and the maintenance of a "simple, honest, effective government"—promises which he had kept faithfully. . . .

During his two and a half years of administration, Governor-General Murphy improved the economic and social aspects of Filipino life. He humanized the Islands' penal code by introducing the indeterminate sentence and the probation system and revising the parole system. He promoted the social welfare of the masses by giving relief to typhoon victims and indigent families, by fighting the evils of city slums and unemployment, by creating the posts of public defenders to defend the poor in the courts, and by founding puericulture and health centers in the rural districts. Moreover, he balanced the budget and placed Philippine finances on a very sound basis, a remarkable feat indeed because most countries at that time, including the United States, were experiencing deficits owing to the worldwide depression.

Murphy's record as governor-general was seldom surpassed in the history of colonial administration. "None of his predecessors," said President Quezon, "can excel him in sympathetic understanding of our problems. No American has ever landed on these shores who had a more sincere affection for the Filipino people, a better appreciation of their virtues, more faith in their abilities, or a greater interest in their welfare."

A further constitutional step along the path toward ultimate independence was the promulgation in February, 1935, of a new constitution which granted general suffrage in the Philippines. When the government provided under this constitution took office at the end of that year, the Commonwealth of the Philippines was established and a thorough reorganization of the administration was begun. The policy of eventual self-government for the Philippines pursued by the United States was rudely shattered in the early hours of December, 8, 1941 when Davao City in Mindanao was bombed by Japanese planes. After a brief campaign the Japanese invaders entered Manila, and on January 3, 1942, proclaimed the establishment of a Japanese military administration. During three years of occupation the Japanese played an important role in stimulating the forces of nationalism in the Philippines, as, indeed, they did in all of the conquered countries of Southeast Asia.

5

NATIONAL REACTION TO COLONIALISM
IN SOUTHEAST ASIA

It has often been said that Western colonialism carried within it
the seeds of its own destruction. Once motives of economic and
political self-interest began to be infused by humanitarian ideals
aimed at improving the welfare of the indigenous peoples, forces
were generated within the Southeast Asian societies which the
colonial powers were unable to control. It is no coincidence that
the famous declaration by the Queen of the Netherlands in 1901
announcing the introduction in Indonesia of the so-called Ethical
Policy ("The Netherlands have a moral duty to fulfill towards the
people of the Indies") should have been followed so soon afterwards
by the establishment of bodies such as *Budi Utomo,* or High En-
deavor organization, which within a year had enrolled many thousands of members in its struggle to obtain improved educational
opportunities for Indonesians. This was followed shortly afterwards
by the establishment of an organization known as *Sarekat Islam,*
which placed its emphasis on the economic and intellectual well-
being of Indonesians as well as on the promotion of Islamic teaching. From these incipient nationalist movements, with their vaguely
defined objectives, grew the hard-core political parties aiming at the
overthrow of the colonial regime. In Indonesia the first Asian Communist Party (PKI) was founded in 1920, and Sukarno's Indonesian
Nationalist Party (PNI) was formed seven years later. The banning
by the Dutch authorities of the PKI after an abortive rebellion in
1926 and the reluctance of the Netherlands government to grant

measures of political reform inevitably led the Indonesian Nationalist Party to develop revolutionary tendencies. Again the Dutch acted decisively, and during the 1930s most of the important Indonesian nationalist leaders were either imprisoned or removed from areas where they derived their political support.

The Dutch were by no means unique in adopting such measures. The British, who expressed their intention of granting ultimate independence to India, were obliged to deal in a similarly repressive manner with leaders of the Indian National Congress Party, which itself gave inspiration to the nationalist independence movement in Burma. In the Philippines the Spanish authorities dealt even more ruthlessly with the national revolutionaries, executing in December, 1896, the "Father of Filipino Nationalism," Dr. Jose Rizal. They were, however, unable to contain the revolution led by Emilio Aguinaldo, who became the first president of the new national revolutionary government. In Indo-China France also faced a growing challenge from the Vietnamese-led nationalist movement after the First World War, and, when it entered a terrorist and rebellious phase in the late 1920s, the French colonial authorities reacted with great severity.

The response of the Western colonial powers to the nationalist challenge varied from country to country and was itself largely conditioned by the objectives of, and the methods employed by, the nationalists themselves. As the following selections show, the opposition to Western colonialism was by no means uniform in the countries of Southeast Asia.

20. Malay-Indonesian Nationalism: A Comparison

The following selection, which presents a comparison between the nationalist movements in Malaya and Indonesia, is extracted from an article by a young Malaysian historian Radin Soenarno in the Journal of Southeast Asian History (*I, 1, 1960, pp. 22-28*). *Reprinted by permission.*

It is generally accepted that the Malay and the Indonesian nationalist movements began as a reaction against the encroachment upon their respective spheres of life by the new, twentieth century alien population, especially the Europeans and the Chinese. In Malaya this reaction started in about 1926 when the first Malay association was formed. In Indonesia it started very much earlier— in 1908 when the first party which was 'purely cultural and social' was founded. In Malaya the 'social and cultural' aspect or phase of the movement lasted till 1937 when quasi-political parties sprang up. In Indonesia it took only four years to reach the political stage. In 1912 the first fully political party emerged from the earlier *SAREKAT DAGANG ISLAM* which was formed but one year previously. From 1912 onwards the Indonesian movement never looked back, but proceeded step by frustrating step towards the achievement of political independence. Its growth was spectacular and its strife was dramatic. Malay nationalism, on the other hand, was full of caution in its progress. Its growth was so slow that it gave the impression that nationalism among the Malays was an evolutionary rather than a revolutionary attitude. It showed more drags and reluctance than drive and eagerness, and in this was very different to Indonesian nationalism.

The slow growth towards political maturity was even conceded by one of their leaders, Tengku Ahmad, the founder-President of the Pahang Malay Association, when he said in his inaugural speech on 21 March 1938, "Although the movement is a little late in coming—if we take full cognizance of our material backwardness—we still have time to make up past deficiencies." There were several factors that explained this 'timid' nature of the nationalist movement in Malaya. According to Ishak Haji Mohammad,

> The failure of the movement (during the pre-war days) can be attributed to the lack of really sincere, daring and honest leaders among the Malays. Usually the choice of leadership then fell on prominent government servants even if they had little qualification for leadership in any movement. Even if they had the necessary qualifications, they had not the adequate time to pay attention to the national need, and perhaps because of their position, they took little notice of the condition of the people.

Ishak made a pertinent observation on the leadership of the Malay nationalist movement. Malay nationalism, though pioneered by the Arabic educated, was essentially a child of English education. The movement derived its leadership mainly from the English educated, both foreign and locally trained intelligentsia, and this group sprang chiefly from the Royal families and the families of the Chiefs. The establishment of such exclusive institutions as the Malay College, moreover, ensured to those born with traditional privilege the leadership of the race. This fact was borne out clearly by the first batch of leaders which included Tengku Ahmad in Pahang and Tengku Ismail in Selangor. Both of them were closely related to the Royal Houses of Pahang and Negeri Sembilan respectively. Others, such as Onn in Johore, Dato Husain in Pahang and Tengku Abdul Kadir in Singapore, all came from prominent families which enjoyed traditional respect. The presence of these leaders at the political helm had a 'restraining' effect on political development.

This was the very opposite of the Indonesian leaders. In Indonesia the educated echelon sprang not only from the aristocracy but also from the small Indonesian middle class of merchants, teachers and government servants. Their first national leader, Dr. Wahidin Soedirohusodo, came from a farmer-family but because of his 'exceptional intelligence' he rose up to be a graduate in medicine and later emerged as a national leader. Other well-known leaders, such as Soekarno himself, who is a son of a village school teacher, and Tan Malaka, the famous Moscow trained communist leader, came from insignificant families. Thus there was a tendency among the Indonesian leaders to be more revolutionary than those in Malaya, for they felt more free from the shackles of traditionalism than their Malayan counterparts.

However the main reason that gave rise to this difference in the rate of growth was the fact that Malay nationalism was still embodied in the feudal social structure. It was more a case of a new wine in an old bottle. The defeudalization process affected mainly the spiritual side of the Malays and only to a very limited extent did it affect the social leadership in a physical sense. The erosion of the traditional leadership by the rise of those not born within the circle of traditional leaders was yet just beginning before the Second World War. In Indonesia the encroachment upon the traditional field of leadership started in fact at the turn of the Century when the Dutch, for fear of the growing influence of pan-

Islamism, made western education available to the indigenous population. Writing about the development of this new elite in Indonesian society, one writer observed, ". . . it would be possible to view the entire Twentieth Century social history of Indonesia as a gradual lowering of the prestige of the Princes and Regents." The rise of this new elite led to the transfer of the allegiance of the masses from the traditional leaders to the new. This process was given impetus by the "creation of new social strata as a result of the diversification of the economy and the impact of a variety of intellectual influences."

This was not so in Malaya. The 'diversification of economy' in Malaya affected only the alien population and not the Malays— at least not beyond the replacement of bartering with the use of money. The British policy of respecting Malay customs and culture, and of preserving the traditional leaders, had the effect of ossifying the social order, while the shorter period of colonial rule too gave to this process an additional emphasis. The end result of all these factors was that Malay nationalism during the pre-War days was more of an attempt of a feudal society to adapt itself to the new world order of democracy and socialism, rather than a national uprising of a people seeking its political freedom from the domination of others.

The dearth of truly nationalistic leaders, comparable to those in Indonesia, was openly deplored by the Malays. Tengku Ismail, in his inaugural speech as the President of the Selangor Malay Association said,

> . . . we all lack leaders who can lead us to national salvation.
> It is with the view to seeking leaders for the future that this Association is founded to-day. This Association will send Malays for higher studies in Egypt and Europe. When they finish their studies they will return to Malaya as the leaders of our children and grand-children. Then only will we be free from this oppression and 'milking' by these foreign races in our Country.

In the light of this statement the Malay nationalist struggle was, therefore, still in the 'beginning stage' by 1938. It had not really entered into the political arena, but was still in the process of preparing to do so. By then the Indonesian nationalist movement had become already a formidable challenger to the Dutch Colonial

Government. It had attempted to overthrow the Government by force in the Communist revolts of 1925 and 1926, and had threatened it by the mass movement under Soekarno in 1928 when the first attempt proved abortive.

In their respective political aims, the Indonesian nationalists sought after the political independence of the country as early as possible. This aim was first adopted by *SAREKAT ISLAM* as early as 1914. The nationalist leaders even dared to choose to co-operate with the [authorities] only when they considered it to be politically advantageous to do so. The Malayan leaders on the other hand, looked upon the Government as the architect of their national destiny. They looked up to it for help and protection against the alien pressure. As a result, their political aim was comparatively unambitious. In 1930 the Raja Muda of Perak, at a dinner given in his honour in London, said,

> I think the present form of government is really the best for the Country (Malaya) and its people. I will not say it is perfect; but if it is not it is trying hard to be so, and I hope it will become perfect in due course. At the present moment every body is contented and happy; although, of course, I have heard a few people, whom I call supermen, are crying for a change of government, but I am glad they are in a minority in my Country, and I do not think they are generally liked. The Country is not quite ready for any change of politics yet, and I do not think it will be ready for a good many years to come.

No doubt the Raja Muda was not a political leader; but to the tradition-bound Malays his words ranked second only to the semi-sacred 'Titah' of the Sultans. In 1930 he was very much a national leader to the Malays, and as such he was "speaking the mind of his countrymen." Anyway, such an expression of satisfaction for the existing political order was not a rare one. The [Singapore] *FREE PRESS* noted, "There is nothing particularly new in this for it has been common place knowledge for many years." This attitude was also to be found among the rightist political leaders. Even by 1938, their dissatisfaction had barely begun to be voiced. The political changes aimed at were well advanced in the future. To quote Tengku Ahmad again, ". . . we will all strive together for the success of this movement which is designed to lay the foundation of the welfare of our future generation."

Another arresting feature of the Malay nationalists that made them unique in [that] part of the world, was the paradox that they upheld the feudal social structure. The Indonesian nationalists, and in fact nationalists of other countries in this area, strove to do away with the old social order. In Indonesia the old elite, which was compromised by its exploitative alliance with the Dutch against its own people, became the first and the principal target of the growing nationalism. In fact, it was only after the position of the traditional bureaucracy had been considerably undermined that nationalism made rapid headway. But in Malaya this process was reversed. The rising Malay nationalism exalted the Malay aristocracy and courted royal patronage as far as it was possible. In view of the state of social development of the Malays then this was inevitable. The Malays woke up from their political slumber only to find themselves already left far behind by the other races in their own Country; and, seeing no new materials available for leadership, they had no choice but to accept that which was available. There were obvious points of strength as well as weakness in this. The *FREE PRESS* commented,

> It will not have been overlooked that in Pahang the Association has the blessing of the Sultan—almost certainly an essential point under present conditions—and that Malay Royalty played a prominent part in the inaugural meeting. This in itself must restrict the scope of the Association's work, but it can not be avoided at this juncture. Similarly other leaders are Malays holding prominent posts in government services, which again must impose restrictions on the extent to which they can propose schemes to which the High Commissioner may be opposed, and must curtail criticism of Government action and policy.

Thus the Royal patronage added another impediment on the path of the Malay nationalist political progress. Nationalism, which was usually free from any vested interest, save the very overall interests of the nation, in Malaya became entangled with feudal consideration for vested interest of a particular class. On the credit side, the advantage of this development was that there was comparatively a greater possibility for the Malay masses to unite into a really integrated body. Since there were no radical changes in the social order, Malay nationalism was not faced with the difficulty of having to reconcile the various new social classes as in the Indonesian society. The masses, as in days of old, were generally still solidly behind the leaders, and once the latter chose to oppose the Government, as in the case of Malay opposition to the implementation of the Malayan Union Constitution in 1946, the Malays rose to the occasion as an organized body.

Also noteworthy in this respect was the high degree of imperviousness of the Malay people to foreign ideological doctrines. The people in general accepted what the leaders stood for, not without question, of course, when it was necessary, but on the whole they showed considerable solidarity. The few leftists who differed from the rest were mostly immigrants from Indonesia who had not fully become integral members of the Malay community. They were looked upon as strangers, and their leftist ideology was repulsive to the Malays. This accounted for the failure of the leftist ideology to spread widely in Malaya, and the scant attention paid to the leftist activities by the pro-Government Malay nationalists.

The Indonesian nationalist movement had none of these advantages. The upsetting of the old order of the society by local and foreign forces, and the subsequent rise of a new social order, resulted in a 'loosening' of the social body, thus increasing its permeability for all sorts of ideological influences. Consequently there arose a riot in political doctrines and the wellnigh impossibility of achieving any degree of national solidarity comparable to that of the Malay movement. The more politically conscious Indonesians could have presented a far more formidable mass movement than they did, had the leadership not been riddled with ideological differences. But this condition was not obtained and any attempt at a unity on a national basis could only be made during the time of extreme stress during the occupation by the Japanese, and even then the unity achieved could only exist temporarily.

Religion had been an important factor in the national uprising, both in Malaya and Indonesia. In Malaya it was the reformist movement of Islam that awakened the Malay political consciousness. In Indonesia it was the attraction of pan-Islamism that first gave the Indonesians a social binding force. Both the Indonesians and the Malays sought spiritual refuge in, as well as derived inspiration from, Islam. However, the respective roles of Islam in Malayan and Indonesian politics before 1945 showed considerable variation. In Indonesia, Islam, after sparking off Indonesian nationalism, continued to play a dominant role in the nationalist movement. The first political party itself was Islamic in nature, and from the date of its formation till about 1919, Islam enjoyed its political heyday in Indonesia. Besides being merely a theological denomination, Islam also offered "an ideological rationale to those who were restive under alien colonial domination." From 1919 till the outbreak of the War Islam suffered a political eclipse, but it would be erroneous to think that it ceased to play its role altogether during this period. It continued to "act as a catalyst on other revolutionary elements in the crucible of change." Islam regained its importance after the War when political parties based on Islam became more active.

In Malaya, Islam had not played a dominant role in politics. It pioneered Malay nationalism but stopped short in about 1926, when under the economic and political pressures from the alien population, Malay political attitudes became more secularist. The reason being, though Islam was unquestionably the Religion of the Malays, its political doctrine after 1900 apparently underwent a radical change. The deposition of the Caliph by the Turkish nationalists in 1924, shocked, if not annoyed, the comparatively more conservative Malays. To them it was most impious to go against the Caliph or the Sultan, the Shadow of Allah on earth. However convincing the argument in favour of the deposition and however spectacular the subsequent social development in Turkey might be, the Malays remained sceptical of the wisdom of the action, and gradually they lost more and more interest in pan-Islamism. Islam again became a mere religion and ceased to be a political activator. It was not until the post-war period that such parties as the [PARTAI] *ISLAM SE-MALAYA* (Pan Peninsula Islamic Party) emerged.

In the final analysis, therefore, Malay nationalism before 1945 formed a story quite unique in many ways. Its peaceful and 'evolutionary' growth gave the impression that the Malays were still very much asleep politically before the [Second World] War. This, of course, was not the case. Underneath the mantle of feudalism and the calm social surface, complex cultural and socio-economic processes were at work. . . . [They] were not comparable to those similar processes taking place in Indonesia; but they [cannot] by any means be ignored if a true understanding of the post-war Malay political movement [is] to be obtained. After all, the physical manifestation of any nationalist movement was only one of its aspects and not the most important either. Perhaps non-violence was a Malayan virtue, for it was the hall mark of the pre-war history of Malaya; and not even such a significant historical event as the political uprising of the Malays could fail to share it.

21. Nationalist Reaction in Indo-China

In Indo-China the French policy of assimilation had been no more successful in curbing the nationalist forces in the country; indeed, it was often those deeply influenced by French culture and education who formed the spearhead of the nationalist movement. Thus in 1908 the University of Hanoi, which had been founded by the French in the previous year, had to be closed for a long period because of the activities within its precincts of rabid nationalists. This selection is extracted from Professor D. G. E. Hall, A History of South-East Asia (Macmillan and Co., Ltd., London, 1955, pp. 646-648) and reprinted by permission.

The nationalist movement in Indo-China was almost entirely confined to the Vietnamese. They were the most numerous of all peoples of the area, and by 1945 constituted about 75 per cent of a population roughly estimated at 25 millions. They had a tradition of nationalism dating from their long struggle for independence against China. Though their civilization remained predominantly Chinese in character, after independence was achieved in 1939, it was no less their own, and in their expansion southwards into the territories previously held by the Chams and the Khmers —i.e. central and southern Annam and Cochin China—they substituted it for the Indianized culture they found in those areas.

The French established themselves in both Cochin China and Tongking by conquest. In each case it was a long protracted struggle, and when at last forced to give in the Vietnamese never lost the hope that one day the hated foreigner would have to withdraw. Banditry was never stamped out; there were constant plots, which the French put down with heartless severity. The French colonists blamed the liberal policy of [Paul] Beau and [Albert] Sarraut and demanded protection. Japan's victory over Russia in 1905 created a wave of unrest, which came to a head in the Gilbert Chieu conspiracy in the following year. The Young Annamites protested against the Franco-Russian alliance. The intelligentsia, influenced by the writings of Chinese reformers such as K'ang Yu Wei, who advocated the study of Western culture, turned to the study of the French philosophical writers, notably Montesquieu and Rousseau, and flocked to the University of Hanoi when it was founded in 1907. But French measures of repression, including the rounding up of suspects and their imprisonment on Pulo Condore, and the closing of the university, brought what may be considered the first phase of the twentieth-century nationalist movement to an end.

Sarraut's liberal policy during his first tenure of office [1911 to 1914] helped to keep Indo-China relatively quiet during World War I. But France made generous promises which she was not prepared to redeem after the war. She also injured Vietnamese susceptibilities by forcibly recruiting no less than 100,000 of them for war service in Europe. Many of these on their return home brought back subversive ideas. The political prisoners, who had been interned on Pulo Condore, were also stimulated to renewed activities after the war by contacts with Siamese and Chinese revolutionaries. The post-war period therefore saw the rise of political parties. The élite were stirred by the doctrine of self-determination proclaimed by the victorious Allies. Some also took their inspiration from the Indian *swaraj* movement, while others imbibed the teachings of the Cantonese Communists. There was a Constitutionalist Party, led by Bui Quang-chieu, which advocated reform along democratic lines, and a Tongkingese Party, led by Pham Quynh, with a similar programme. The government turned down a programme of mild reform submitted by Pham Quynh. It was then the turn of the extremists to steal the limelight from the moderates.

In 1925 the Revolutionary Party of Young Annam was founded. But the mutual jealousies of its leaders paralysed it, and when its Communist members seceded in 1929 it soon came to grief; for the secessionists informed the police against their former comrades and the party was suppressed. A Tongkingese party calling itself the Nationalist Annamite Party came into being through Kuomintang contracts. Half of its members were in government service. It had a very limited following but hoped for foreign aid. It sought also to win over the Vietnamese battalions in the army. In January 1929 it made an unsuccessful attempt to assassinate Governor [Pierre] Pasquier, and in the following month killed Bazin, the head of the Labour Bureau. Its terrorist activities brought the police so hot on its trail that it was forced to launch a rebellion with inadequate preparations. This began with the abortive Yen-bay mutiny of February 1930, and there were outbreaks of violence in many places. The French reacted with the most tremendous severity. Every kind of manifestation, even unarmed demonstrations, was broken up by force, and so many of its leaders were arrested that the party dissolved.

The ferocity of the suppression of the extremist outbreaks of 1930 forced Communism underground. The small party which numbered some 1,500 members in 1931, was ably led by Nguyen-Ai-Quoc, better known as Ho Chi Minh. He had joined the Communist Party in France before the First World War. After the armistice he went to Russia, where he studied revolutionary technique. Then in Canton he founded the Association of Revolutionary Annamite Youth. It was composed of revolutionaries who went there for training at the Wampoa Academy. His aim was the nationalist one of winning Vietnamese independence. On his own showing this was to be accomplished through a democratic bourgeois regime; Communism was to be introduced at a later stage. He drew up a programme which appealed to intellectuals and peasants alike. It included the reduction of fiscal burdens, the redistribution of land among the peasantry, and the abolition of the conscription of labourers and native soldiers for service abroad.

Self-effacing as a leader, he was a strict disciplinarian. Where other leaders and their parties failed, his firm, intelligent leadership succeeded; and although he was arrested by the British in Hong Kong and imprisoned for three years, his movement persisted against all attempts by the French to extirpate it. In 1939 it became Viet Minh, or the League for the Independence of Vietnam. During the period of the Japanese occupation it was to become the spearhead of the nationalist movement. Thus while in the pre-war period Vietnamese nationalism as a movement was ineffective, and weakened by personal or local jealousies and rivalries, it was to find a new life under the direction of a leader of inflexible will and tireless energy. The pity was that French intransigence caused it to fall under Communist leadership. The Vietnamese, with their deep attachment to property and the patriarchal family system, are not natural recruits to Communism.

22. *Some Characteristics of Burmese Nationalism*

In Burma, as the following selection points out, the nationalist movement differed from those in other Southeast Asian countries by being profoundly and uniquely influenced by Buddhism. The selection is extracted from William L. Holland's introduction to Asian Nationalism and the West (The Macmillan Company, New York, 1953, pp. 33-38) *and reprinted by permission.*

The example of Burma provides some illuminating and distinctive aspects of modern Asian nationalism. Much more than Ceylon, Burma has been profoundly influenced in its nationalist evolution by the Buddhist faith. The earliest manifestations of modern Burmese nationalism were first reflected in the activities of Burma's Buddhist monks (*pongyis*). Inspired, as were some other Asian countries, by Japan's victory over Russia in 1905, numerous Young Men's Buddhist Associations (YMBA) were founded in the succeeding years. Originally concerned with promoting a revival of interest in Burma's cultural and religious past, these associations soon engaged in political activities and became a leading political force in the country. They were transformed after the first world war into the General Council of Buddhist Associations (GCBA), or

Wunthanu, which was somewhat modelled on the Indian National Congress and which, organizing its political activities around a minimum program of home rule, boycotted elections and refused to participate in the British-sponsored governments. The earliest secular nationalist political parties developed out of the GCBA, and close ties between Buddhism and nationalist political movements continued into the 1930's.

The existence of the vernacular monastic schools throughout Burma were a key element in the strength of Buddhist influence. Each village had such a school which Buddhist tradition required every boy to attend for some period at least, and which were responsible for the high degree of male literacy in Burma. Though accepted for basic education on the primary school level, the large majority of these schools were not incorporated into the government-regulated system of education, received no government financial assistance, and tended to be overshadowed by the lay and missionary-sponsored schools developed under the British. In 1939-40, there were estimated to be some 18,000 of these "unrecognised" monastic schools in Burma, with an attendance of 200,000 pupils. Yet the very fact that the Buddhist schools were being pushed into the background tended to set the priesthood against the British. As [J. S.] Furnivall notes (in a lecture given in 1952), the British system of education "provided lay schools which enabled boys to pass through the standards and qualify for a job more rapidly. Education was debased from a social to an economic asset. Under this economic stimulus the wealthier and abler boys deserted the monastic schools, and the monastic schools deteriorated. This deprived the monastic order of one of its chief social functions. Religion was thrust back into the middle ages and became a stronghold of reactionary national sentiment. The members of the order had good reason to resent the decline of their former influence, and many became active opponents of the Government. Thus religion was distorted to serve the cause of nationalism, and one of the chief troubles during the later years was the disorderly conduct of the monastic order."

Aggressive, politically-active *pongyis* thus played a key role in prewar Burmese nationalist politics. Local leaders of the *Wunthanu* (GCBA), for example, were active in the "Saya San" rebellion of

1930-31 in lower Burma, a rural uprising which, though ostensibly directed principally at the Indian Chettyar money-lenders, became a serious movement working for the overthrow of British rule. Most of the leading prewar parties and politicians had close associations with monks. Even the leaders of the Thakin party, a predominantly Marxist-oriented organization of young Burmese intellectuals founded in the mid-1930's, accepted Buddhism as a major component of Burmese culture, though they were free from the direct influence of the priesthood itself. The Thakin party, with a political program of immediate and complete freedom for Burma, and a radical economic reform program, was the precursor of the Anti-Fascist People's Freedom League (AFPFL), which won Burmese independence, as well as of the Communist and Socialist parties. In the postwar period, Buddhism has continued to be a major force in Burmese life. The date set for Burmese independence (January 4, 1948) is reported to have been recommended by astrologers. Premier U Nu (formerly known as Thakin Nu), a Socialist who succeeded Aung San as leader of the AFPFL, is a devout Buddhist, and a Buddhist revival is apparently being encouraged, partially as an additional weapon against the influence of the Communists.

The character of Burmese nationalism has been much influenced by the fact that about four million of the over seventeen million population of Burma consist of minorities such as the Kachins, the Chins, and the Karens. Though most of these minorities live in hilly frontier regions surrounding the central plains of the country, a great number of the Karens have moved into the latter area. They have tended, however, to maintain their separate identity, and Christian missionaries have had a strong influence among them. When most of the Burmese refused to participate in the former government, the British enlisted Karen, as well as Indian and Chinese, support. The Karens also were an important source of manpower for the British-controlled military establishment. The long-standing animosity between the Karens and the Burmese flared up during the Japanese campaign of conquest in Burma, during which some Burmese forces are reported to have killed and looted among the Karens. The legacy of hostility continued into the postwar period when many Karens were considered to be less anxious than the Burmese for independence. Though promised an important degree of autonomy within the Burma Union, the more militant of the Karens took up arms against the new government, and later set up their own state, "Kawthulay," at Toungoo. . . .

Equally important has been the influential position of Burma's alien minorities. In the prewar period, over a million Indians and 200,000 Chinese resided in the country. While the British held the top rungs of the economic ladder, Indians played a leading role in business and agriculture, the Madras Chettyar banking caste holding a dominant position in agricultural finance. Indian laborers, willing to work at cheaper wages than Burmans, were also becoming predominant in the Rangoon labor market just before the war, when Indians constituted some 45 per cent of the city's population. The Chinese had a position of some influence in mercantile and mining activities but were less important economically than the Indians, and not nearly as much disliked by the Burmans. Anti-Indian resentment in the prewar period was a vital element in the development of Burmese nationalism. As already indicated, the "Saya San" rebellion had a definite anti-Indian character and was in turn followed by the serious anti-Indian riots of 1938. The British were often blamed by Burma's nationalist leaders for allowing unrestricted Indian immigration, and economic exploitation by Indians. Drastic restriction of Indian immigration was always an important part of the Burmese nationalists' political program.

Some 400,000 Indians, including most of the Chettyars, fled Burma at the time of the Japanese invasion, but in postwar years relatively few have returned. The new Burmese government has indicated its determination to prevent any large revival of Indian immigration, and to place severe limitations on Indian economic activities within Burma. Strong action along these lines, however, seems to have been held in abeyance, partly because of protests from India. However, large numbers of Indian civil servants in Burma have been dismissed and the Indian grip on the Burmese economy has been greatly weakened. Other outstanding unsettled questions are the problem of compensation to the Chettyars, whose lands in Burma were taken over, and the adjustment of Burma's national debt owed to India from pre-independence days.

It should be emphasized, however, that despite the existence of such potential sources of hostility between the two countries and the strong disposition of the Indian government to support its nationals abroad, official relations between the two governments have thus far remained generally cordial.

Paradoxically, though Burmese nationalism has had an important anti-Indian content, it has at the same time leaned on India to advance its own nationalist objectives. Burma was attached to India after its conquest by the British, and the Burmans consistently demanded application to Burma of the new concessions won from the British by the more powerful Indian nationalist movement. They thus demanded that they be included in the post-World War I reform program for India (the Government of India Act of 1919 which, as a result of these demands, was extended to Burma in 1921), and in the succeeding two decades were granted an increasingly autonomous administration, paralleling the limited constitutional reforms conferred on India. When a separation of Burma from India was recommended by the Simon Commission in 1930 (and implemented in the Government of Burma Act of 1935), leading Burman nationalist leaders opposed such a separation, even though it provided for a larger degree of self-government than before, for fear that British promises to India of eventual full self-government would not now be applied to Burma. (The separation proposal was actually rejected by the Burma electorate in 1932, but it nevertheless went into effect in 1937, under the terms of the Government of Burma Act of 1935).[1] Also, as already noted, the organization of the *Wunthanu* (GCBA) was inspired to an important extent by the example of the Indian National Congress.

In the postwar period as well, it was the success of Indian nationalism in achieving the removal of British power that essentially determined the British decision to leave Burma. U Kyaw Myint, head of the Burmese delegation to the Asian Relations Conference in 1947, thus told the Indians, "You are now about to be free. We have always had the good luck to be able to follow your example with very little effort. Because you are about to be free, we are about to be free. However," he added, "we have also contributed our little mite."

To a remarkable degree prewar Burma lacked an indigenous

[1] See Selection 17.

business class. In [J. S.] Furnivall's words, "All that stood for the modern world in Burma, commerce, industry, communication and the modern professions of medicine and engineering, were in foreign hands." The modern educated Burmans were almost all lawyers, journalists, clerks or government employees, many of whom gravitated naturally towards politics. These developments made for two kinds of nationalist politics. One was an opportunist type, with no real popular base, characteristic of most post-1937 parties and governments in Burma. The other type, represented originally by the Thakins, adopted a very radical program and developed links with peasant and labor groups. This situation was also a contributing factor to the "radical" character of all Burmese nationalism, particularly of the Marxist-influenced Thakin group. This characteristic was evident in the postwar period, too, when all but the discredited "rightist" politicians of prewar days talked in Marxist terms. The new government itself immediately announced socialist economic plans, including the proposed nationalization of foreign enterprise, and even talked, in a Two-Year Plan adopted in 1948, of investigating the possibility of eventual collectivization of agriculture.

A deep-rooted tradition of violence has long been apparent in the rural life and the nationalist movements of Burma. It was aggravated by the breakdown of social and economic stability in the countryside, primarily due to the rapid commercialization of agriculture under British rule, with the creation of a landless, transient agricultural laborer class, and general rural dissatisfaction. This problem was tremendously accentuated by the economic depression of the 1930's which brought a catastrophic fall in rice prices. By 1936 the Chettyar money-lenders alone owned outright approximately one quarter of the ten million acres of Lower Burma paddy land and held mortgages on perhaps a million and a half more. By 1939, fifty-nine per cent of the agricultural land in Lower Burma and thirty-two per cent in Upper Burma was leased, and forty to seventy per cent of the tenants were reported to be changing holdings after less than three years of occupancy. The growing distress of this landless, debt-ridden rural population became a major factor in the remarkable growth of banditry in rural Burma.

Many Buddhist monks took an active role in the rural areas in gaining peasant support for their own nationalist aims; and the Thakin party, in the late 1930's, organized numerous peasant unions and created a strong rural component of their political activities. The wartime AFPFL and its National Army were largely recruited in the countryside, as was Aung San's postwar paramilitary organization, the People's Volunteer Organization (PVO). The presence of ample Japanese and Allied arms in Burma as a legacy of the war also contributed to the continued postwar violence in the countryside, some of it politically controlled and directed, but much of it simple dacoity (armed gang robbery). The various dissident movements today are based to a large extent on this rural instability, which is likely to remain a threat to national unity until the more pressing social and economic problems of the countryside have been resolved. Though Burma's independence was "peacefully" negotiated, the existence of armed forces and groups, all opposed to British rule and operating largely from a countryside completely out of control, was a decisive factor in the victory of Burma's nationalist movement. This spirit of violence was reflected in the remark of a Burmese delegate at the 1947 Asian Relations Conference: "I have the deepest possible respect and admiration for Mahatma Gandhi. At the same time I have to say that the Burmese are a nation of fighters."

23. Filipino Nationalist Response to Western Colonialism

This selection, which gives an admirable account of the Filipino nationalist response to Western colonialism, has been extracted from an article on the subject by Professor O. D. Corpuz, himself a Filipino, in the Journal of Southeast Asian History *(III, 1, 1962, pp. 16-21) and is reprinted by permission.*

It was impossible for the Filipinos to regard themselves as one nation until after the middle of the XIXth century. They were scattered by geography, kept apart from each other by a backward technology, distracted from an awareness of their disunity by a system of "monkish education", and politically isolated by Spanish colonial policy. It is true, in some sense, that they were members of a political community, the Spanish colonial community in the Philippines, and that they were members of one ecclesiastical body, the communion of Roman Catholic believers. Doubtless during the XVIth and XVIIth centuries, at the height of their success, the invincibility and prosperity of the political and ecclesiastical systems appealed to the native subjects, and evoked in them some pride in the opportunity to share in some of the Hispanic ideals. Nevertheless, the dominant elements in these two systems were alien first and last; the Filipinos were for centuries regarded by the Spanish political superiors as subjects, and by the Spanish ecclesiastics as a flock of immature and sinful wards.

Suddenly, in the XIXth century, Spain received the delayed but potent impact of the French Enlightenment. There was a violent revolution in ideas, and the old order began to reel before the ideals of secularism, popular sovereignty, national self-determination, and individual liberty. Spanish politics became an un-ending crisis as the ideals of constitutionalism and liberal republicanism battled with the interests of absolute monarchy. The struggle was indecisive in Spain, but every victory of constitutionalism or republicanism in Madrid led to measures of political and economic liberalism in Manila. Here, intellectual and economic liberty, though never complete, produced ideological aspirations and bolstered economic interests; a native intelligentsia developed, oriented to liberalism, and enabled by varying degrees of prosperity and determination to travel to Europe and the European cities of mainland Asia.

Everywhere the Filipino intellectuals were eye-witnesses to the decay of the old order. The Spanish political community irretrievably lost its aura of invincibility, and the ecclesiastical community its halo of finality. It is now the last quarter of the century. The Filipino intellectual could no longer relate himself to systems which had lost their authority; yet because his consciousness had by now transcended his little town and village, it became necessary, above and before anything else, to relate himself to a community. The Filipino intellectual had to identify himself.

This is the beginning of nationalism as a dynamic factor in the history of the Filipino. The problem of self-identification was solved by the peoples of Europe and America by the decision, sometimes of the mind but more often of the heart, that they constituted a national community. This decision is the great act of self-discovery or re-discovery, which immediately defines a people's perspectives, and creates bonds of affection among them.

The ideal of the Filipino national community, first an unsure hope among the intellectuals of the 1870s and 1880s, was communicated in sharpened form by the propaganda of the 1890s to the masses of the Filipinos. Almost overnight the intellectuals and the masses created symbols for *their* national community. This ideological and moral estrangement between the Filipinos and the Spanish colonial community now provided the dynamic ideals for the Filipinos who had been socially alienated from Spanish colonial institutions. The Revolution of 1896 followed, and the Empire died in 1898.

The triumph of the nationalist revolution, however, was short-lived. America came into the picture at this point, and dealt the death-blow not only to the Spanish Empire, but also the Filipino Republic of 1898.

The United States occupation of the [Philippines] was, generally, a half-century of compromise.[1] It was a compromise between the grand tradition of Empire on the one hand, and the fiery ideals of nationalism on the other. The Spanish-American war was soon followed by hostilities between the Filipinos and Americans which, fought along the lines of guerilla warfare, was a long-drawn out affair (1899-1902), was expensive to both sides, and was marked by well-publicised severities and atrocities. The deterioration of the Philippine situation, which was exploited articulately by the Democratic opposition in the United States, was probably the main factor in bringing about a sobering reaction to the enthusiastic jingoism that had plunged America into the war with Spain. The claims of Empire came thereby to be moderated by a new, and sober, colonial morality.

In the colonial administration, this moderated imperialism was manifested by policies of accommodation to the Filipinos. Important positions in the colonial government were given to the Filipino upper class, which thereby strengthened its conservative outlook and tendencies. Employment opportunities which were generated

[1] See Selection 19.

by harmonious relations between government and business interests created a Filipino middle class, which was soon to take advantage of a public educational system that trained them for lower positions in the colonial bureaucracy, and, which is just as significant, gave them a large dose of civic education that was oriented to American ideals. The colonial regime, however, wisely attracted the nationalists by extending recognition to the heroism of Jose Rizal, the Filipino patriot who was executed by the Spaniards (1896). Finally, in contrast to the Spaniards, the Americans embarked on constructive measures in the fields of public works, health and sanitation, and technological development.

The moderation of the colonialists was reciprocated in equal measure by the nationalists. This was partly because of the success of the social programs of the colonial regime. These programs, which were accompanied by economic prosperity, were implemented under a fortuitous combination of advantageous circumstances. In the first place, social progress during this period served, by the contrast it offered to the Spanish record of neglect, to reflect credit upon the Americans. Secondly, social progress took place at a rate and on a scale which did not immediately produce the dislocations and social conflicts of the post-1945 period. Exception, however, might be made here of the localised peasant uprisings of the 1930s in the rice and sugar *haciendas* north of Manila. Thirdly, social progress was, after all, recognised as a part of the aims and purposes of the nationalist movement.

But perhaps the decisive reason for the moderation of Filipino nationalism was the fact that the Filipino political and economic elite had been coopted into the colonial regime. Indeed, high American officials took a leading role in the organisation of the *Partido Federal,* composed of wealthy Filipinos, which had a platform based on annexation of the Philippines as a state in the Union. For a time, all important government appointments to Filipinos were given to members of this party. The policy of accommodation proved to be immensely successful. The leading families took over the leadership in the Filipino participation in the colonial government. The participation was substantial, and extended to all levels and branches of the administration. This cooptation naturally invested the Filipino leadership with some share of responsibility for the success of the colonial regime. Witnessing, therefore, the abundant signs of social and political progress among their people, a progress which was evidently the product of co-operation between the Americans and themselves, the Filipino na-tionalists soon learned to look at nationalism and colonialism in a new light. Filipino independence remained the political battle-cry of the dominant *Nacionalista* party, but the *Nacionalistas* in more than three decades of power (1907-1941) had developed political interests that seemed joined to those of the colonial power. They also developed a cautious attitude toward the risks to the Philip-pines that were implied by a change of status from protected de-pendency to independent statehood. In order to rationalise their cautious conservatism, the Filipino leadership therefore upheld the argument that the sentiments and ideals of the nationalist revolu-tion of 1896 were actually being realised within the framework of harmonious relations with the colonial power. Thus, at least for the moment, emerged a reconciliation of nationalism and colonial-ism, and the Filipino leaders adopted policies of pragmatic and conservative nationalism.

After the peaceful transfer of power that marked the assumption of sovereignty in 1946, however, came the need to redefine the basis of Filipino-American relations. There were three basic issues: (a) America's obligations in connection with the postwar rehabilita-tion of the Philippines, (b) post-independence economic relations, and (c) mutual defence arrangements.

The first was an issue because of the Filipino complaint that [America] had not made good on President Roosevelt's war-time promise to completely rehabilitate Philippine war damage. This complaint was aggravated by the observation that former enemy countries such as Japan seemed to be receiving favored-nation treatment. The problem of economic relations was less sentimental, but equally serious. The Filipino economy had become during the colonial period a two- or three-crop (Manila hemp, copra, sugar) ex-port economy which was precariously dependent on free entry into the American market. The tariffs and other duties implied by Phil-ippine independence threatened to kill off these dollar-earning in-dustries. The United States Congress decided to levy graduated tariffs on Filipino products over a 20-year period, during which time Filipino export industries were supposed to complete adjustments to the competitive conditions of the world market. The Congress, however, tied this to a requirement that the Filipinos amend their Constitution in order to grant equal or "parity" rights to Americans in the exploitation of Philippine natural resources, and in the conduct of business enterprises. The Filipinos had no choice but to amend their Constitution, for the alternative was national economic ruin. The American requirement was consequently resented as an unfair imposition and as a violation of Filipino sovereignty. The mutual defence arrangements have also been sharply criticised as giving certain unilateral advantages to the United States, and the issue is unavoidably complicated by the frictions generated by the presence of military installations and troops on Filipino soil.

These issues, understandably, are among the leading "irritants" in postwar Filipino-American relations. But perhaps more important is the observation of Senator Claro M. Recto, the redoubtable critic of our relations with America: that the American position on each of these issues indicates that the national interests of a country are best promoted and protected by itself. It is against this background of Filipino-American relations, and against the lesson that the defence of Filipino interests must be entrusted to Filipinos, that the basic sentiment of nationalism has re-emerged with fresh vigor in the Philippines. The habits of mind that had proved so successful during the colonial relationship seemed inappropriate for an independent nation. It became necessary, therefore, to formulate a definition of the Filipino national interest.

It is doubtful whether such a definition has been achieved. On the surface, all the postwar administrations have sought popular support for policies which they have invariably labelled as nationalistic. This political style has been followed most strikingly by the current majority party, which has coined the slogan of "Filipino First" for its approach to domestic and foreign policy questions. This slogan has been implemented, at least on the legislative level, through statutes "nationalising" some professions and industries and granting priority in the allocation of scarce foreign exchange to Filipinos. Numerous other bills would extend the application of Filipino First to the staffing of the churches, as well as of private school institutions. However, one doubts whether the reserving of certain social enterprises and occupations to nationals, which is so far the meaning of Filipino First, is the essential meaning of nationalism.

The younger generation in the Filipino electorate is still inadequately represented in the higher ranks of the political leadership, relative to the generation which was dominant in the era of compromise with colonialism. This earlier generation continues to dominate the highest executive, legislative, and judicial positions. While there is reason to believe that the change in the age structure of the voting population will lead to change in national political outlook, the directions of change are at the moment vague and uncertain. Another complicating factor is the universality with which nationalism has been embraced as a political slogan. So long as factions with known, and sharp, divergences in political ambitions and economic interests all profess a devoted adherence to nationalism, it will remain a slogan rather than become a differentiating ideology in national politics. Then, too, Filipino politics is notorious for the ideological shallowness of the leading parties' programs and pronouncements. Perhaps this is traceable to the common class origins of the traditional political leadership, and to the fact that the top political leaders in the post-1946 era (except the late Ramon Magsaysay) all belonged to the single dominant *Nacionalista* party of the American period. The fact that the pre-war *Nacionalistas* have split into two rival factions (Liberals and *Nacionalistas*) which will shortly be taken over by a new generation of leaders promises to produce differences in ideological orientation. Nevertheless, the present is a period of transition in Filipino politics, and time, plus probable political re-alignments, are needed to clarify the situation.

6

NATIONAL INDEPENDENCE:
THE JAPANESE CATALYST

Perhaps no other single event in the modern history of Asia has had such a profound influence on the subsequent course of events as the defeat of Russia by Japan in 1905. For the first time it was demonstrated conclusively that an Asian power, using the Western implements and engines of war, could master a European nation. The moral did not have to be spelled out to Asian intellectuals, who were inspired by the resurgence of the new Asia as represented by Japan. The defeat did much to bolster incipient nationalist fervor in Southeast Asia and gave to its leaders confidence in challenging the political control of the Western powers. Indeed, one of the most important but least understood elements inhibiting the growth of nationalist feeling in Southeast Asia during the twentieth century lay at what can only be described as the psychological level: the engrained sense of inferiority engendered by Western political and economic domination. It was at this hidden level that the defeat of Russia by the Japanese made its impact.

And just as it was the Japanese who taught their fellow Asians this important lesson at the beginning of the twentieth century, so it was the Japanese who provided the occasion for the Southeast Asian nationalists to seize power, sometimes after bitter struggle, during the mid-1940s after a bloody world conflict. It is therefore ironical that, although the Japanese, by driving the Western colonial powers from the Philippines, Indo-China, Burma, Malaya, and Indonesia, acted as the catalyst in the formation of the new nation states of Southeast Asia, they were not themselves, except perhaps initially, regarded as liberators by the Southeast Asian peoples, for they imposed an even more hateful brand of colonialism, as embodied in the East Asia Co-Prosperity Sphere.

24. The Japanese Period in Southeast Asian History

The significance of the Japanese overlordship in generating the forces of nationalism and national liberation has been well summarized by Professor Harry J. Benda in an article, "The Structure of South East Asian History," published in the Journal of Southeast Asian History *(III, 1, 1962, pp. 133-138) and reprinted here by permission.*

It can be convincingly argued that the demise of Western colonialism in the early 1940's should form the terminal point for the study of Southeast Asian history, since the destruction of the colonial *status quo* directly led to the subsequent, and still contemporary, era of revolution, liberation and modern nationhood. I would, instead, plead that the Japanese interregnum be provisionally accorded the status of a distinct historical epoch in Southeast Asian history. I disagree with the almost generally prevailing notion that that interregnum was no more than a superficial (because brief) episode which can be conveniently and adequately relegated to a preface to present-day Southeast Asia. Whatever its significance for post-war developments, the Japanese occupation differed from them in the one, but crucial, respect that Southeast Asian history during those short but eventful years was to a large extent still made, or at least decisively influenced, by aliens. Only after 1945 do Southeast Asians, to varying degrees, once again determine their own fate, in part at least by continuing, or conversely by reacting against, the twin legacies of Western and Japanese overlordship. It is, indeed, no exaggeration to say that without the Japanese interlude, the balance between continuity and change in contemporary Southeast Asia might conceivably still be weighted in favor of continuity, or at best of more gradual, evolutionary change. Japanese rule, moreover, was not merely a period of military occupation. In many ways, the Japanese wittingly or unwittingly interfered in virtually all aspects of Southeast Asian life, albeit to different extents in the various countries, and to different degrees in areas occupied by Army and Navy, respectively. If only as a catalyst, then, the last stage of foreign domination fully deserves—in spite of great gaps in available documentation—careful attention as a significant stage in the history of Southeast Asia.

A full understanding of the effects of Japanese rule has to commence with the observation that its short-run *raison d'être* differed profoundly from the purposes of modern Western colonial rule. (The contours of peacetime colonial rule by a victorious Japan can, of course, only be the subject of conjecture). The exigencies and demands of the war seemingly dictated a twin policy of ensuring, by whatever means, internal peace and order while extracting the maximum benefits in terms of material and human resources from the occupied territories. In the process of enforcing these policies, the occupying power for better or worse rode roughshod over much that Western colonialism had created, whether in the Westernized sector of the economy, the precarious advances in social welfare and social engineering in general, and, last but not least, in political liberalization. To a large extent, that is to say, Japanese rule constituted a calculated or unintentional reversal, and often a destruction, of the colonial order, here and there accompanied by perhaps equally important endeavours at Japanizing the occupied countries. The careful administration by trained colonial experts suddenly gave way to often crude improvisation by military personnel or militarized bureaucrats without adequate academic or administrative training. While—particularly in the early stages of the occupation—concern for internal, indigenous problems occupied a secondary place in Japanese plans, Japanese actions almost from the outset affected Southeast Asian societies to a marked degree, and often far beyond the intentions of Japan's policy makers at home and in the occupied regions. In several respects, the occupation era was thus, not unlike modern Western colonialism, subject to internal contradictions.

My greatest concern here is . . . with the most important structural changes which Nipponese domination effected within the framework of earlier social relationships, particularly those created in the modern colonial period. . . . These were on the whole more conspicuous in formerly 'directly' administered areas where the demise of Western colonialism had led to a partial socio-political vacuum which the Japanese proceeded to fill by various indigenous elite groups. The areas formerly under 'indirect' rule did not, of course, remain unaffected by Japanese policies either, and here and there—notably e.g. in Achin—the interregnum did produce significant changes. Since the traditional ruling classes had been among the main beneficiaries of Western colonial rule, the Japanese seem to have distrusted them *en bloc,* and to have more heavily relied on competing, notably religious, elites. But whatever their early misgivings, the Japanese ultimately came to respect the social *status quo* wherever it was represented by more or less entrenched traditional political, or economic, elites; the *présence Japonique* thus left the fabric of the Malay, Filipino (and of course of the Thai) ruling classes relatively intact. The exceptional case of Vietnam, where nominal French control continued until early 1945, deserves additional study.

In Burma and Java, particularly, where no such significant vested indigenous classes existed, the Japanese from the very outset sought the cooperation of other elite groups, and in fact very considerably aided in their consolidation. The relative strengthening of these groups—notably of the Western-trained, nationalist intelligentsias—should, however, not be misread for a concerted Japanese move to make more than spurious and carefully guarded concessions. The 'rectilinear' interpretation of Southeast Asian nationalism has led to the rather naive view that through lack of numbers and ignorance, if not because of intrinsic weakness, Japanese administrators were forced to allow free play to nationalist sorcerers' apprentices, either as quasi-collaborators or as anti-Japanese resistance fighter[s]. The record would seem to indicate that until almost the end of the occupation (in the case of Burma and the Philippines, until the Allied re-invasion), the Japanese were in undisputed control of internal events; it was they who held the keys to all power, and it was they who rigorously maintained the limits within which urban elites, especially, were allowed to move. Whether nominally exercising the authority of 'independent' governments or whether playing less ele-

the whole the Japanese apparently utilized, revolutionized, and consolidated the religious elites and thus endowed them with potential political strength—both vis-à-vis traditional and nationalist elites—without precedent in modern Southeast Asian history.

The occupation regimes did not only exert decisive influence on the position of already existing social groups, they were also instrumental in creating entirely new ones which soon started to compete for influence, prestige, and—in post-war years—for power with other elites. The most important of these were without doubt the new Southeast Asian military leaders, reared by the Japanese army commands in many parts of the area. While colonial armies had as a rule been drawn from ethnic minorities, and officered by Westerners, the Japanese recruited and trained entire armies and officers' corps from among the major ethnic groups in Southeast Asia. Enthusiastic young men of common birth, but without either religious or Western training—hitherto the exclusive prerequisites for non-aristocratic elite status—eagerly responded to the opportunities to gain social status and prestige thus opened up to them. Side by side with the military proper we find other new leaders emerging from the plethora of youth and other organizations brought into being by the occupying power. Prestigious, if in terms of actual significance perhaps hollow, positions awaited them as auxiliary police, as scout leaders, as aides in the distribution of food and clothing—and as spies for the New Order in villages and towns. These emerging elite groups are of more than only sociological interest, for they represent a veritable re-valuation of traditional social values in Southeast Asia, a concomitant of the revolutionary tide generated by occupation policies and propaganda. Politicized and often militarized during the war years, these young people rapidly developed into a clientele for political, nationalist appeals, into transmission belts between city and countryside, but also into new potential leadership groups challenging older-generation political and religious elites.

For purposes of a thorough analysis of the Japanese interregnum the above brief sketch of structural changes among Southeast Asian elites would have to be supplemented by studies concerning the often equally significant innovations introduced by Japanese rule in other segments of urban and rural societies. Ruth-

vated roles as leaders of as-yet dependent peoples, the scope of
tionalist elites was pitifully restricted, their activities narrowly
cumscribed, and their bargaining power vis-à-vis the occupying p
virtually nonexistent. Much of their weakness was doubtless d
Japanese unwillingness to devolve real codetermination, let
power, on anyone, let alone on partners whose radical, ideol
orientation they had good reason to suspect; far more signifi
the intelligentsias moreover lacked both internal cohesion a
groups proper and, as yet, widespread popular support. Ye
terms of actual power the representatives of Southeast Asian
alism demonstrably gained little while Japanese overlordship
they nonetheless owe to the occupation an immense increase
social and political stature and prestige and a great deal
proved organizational techniques. They had come close en
the fulcrum of politics so that when the war abruptly end
almost inevitably emerged as the best-qualified group
control in the vacuum created by the Japanese surrender,
longed (as in Indonesia) by tardy reoccupation and atter
colonization by the former metropolitan powers.

If the interregnum had brought the urban intelligent
the periphery to the center of public life, it wrought n
portant changes in the status of religious elites in South
With the exception of Indonesia, this aspect of Japane
has so far unfortunately remained relatively neglected.
the peasantry's acquiescence in, if not support for, wartii
was doubtless one of the most crucial Japanese targets,
to win allies among religious leaders flowed logically f
istic understanding of the key role of *pongyi* and *ulam*
haps also of the lower Catholic clergy) in peasant life.
wrongly, the Japanese may moreover have felt that relig
were politically less sophisticated and hence ideological
able than Western-educated intellectuals. In stark co
colonial powers' aloofness vis-à-vis Southeast Asian
Japanese apparently fostered religious organizations,
ing rural and urban religious leaders together in ma
under military or naval control. Their concern for
did not, it is true, altogether obviate the recurrence o
rest under religious, sometimes even anti-Japanese, b

less recruitment of labor battalions and auxiliary soldiers caused displacement of manpower throughout the area without regard to racial or national affiliations. Increasingly heavy pressure on food supplies by the occupation authorities brought untold hardship to many peasants, but it also led to wide-spread squatting on former estate lands in some parts of Southeast Asia. Indigenous societies were, then, subjected to outside pressures of unprecedented vehemence, while at the same time Japanese-sponsored propaganda sought to imprint many new values on broad layers of the population. Add to all this the sudden removal and public humiliation of the former Western overlords, and political and economic encroachments on other segments of the 'plural societies', and the distinct, and truly revolutionary, character of the occupation era will stand out in bold relief. Perhaps the relief is too boldly drawn and should be carefully sieved through the eyes, and the written accounts, of Southeast Asians themselves, to attain a more balanced appraisal of this stage of Southeast Asian history.

25. The Impact of the Japanese Occupation in Malaya

Nowhere was the sudden impact of Japanese occupation more brutally felt than in Malaya, which had for so long been under the paternalistic British regime. The different races of the country— Chinese, Malays, and Indians—all experienced the occupation in different ways, as the following selection makes clear. It is extracted from an essay, "Nationalism in Malaya," by T. H. Silcock and Ungku Abdul Aziz, in Asian Nationalism and the West, *edited by William L. Holland (The Macmillan Company, New York, 1953, pp. 289-298) and reprinted by permission.*

The invasion of Malaya by the Japanese in December 1941 produced many different effects on nationalism in the peninsula. Among the Malays the important effects were shock and upheaval, and also the learning of the habits of violence and of staged mass demonstrations. Among the Chinese the Occupation meant guerrilla activity, a sense of insecurity and a reversion to habits based on personal accommodation to an atmosphere of violence; the psychological effect on their attitude to the British was also very important. Among the Indians the organisation of the Indian Independence League and the Indian National Army was probably the dominant factor. But on all the peoples of Malaya, brought up in an atmosphere in which government had been run by an alien people, on the whole accepted as friendly, and in which politics was definitely not respectable, the sudden change of masters and the impact of violent Japanese nationalism and pan-Asianism was a most intensive school for nationalist feelings and thoughts about political questions.

JAPANESE OCCUPATION METHODS

The principal technique of the Japanese was one of stirring up anti-European feeling emphasizing that they were an Asian people. They were not concerned with efficient or progressive administration. Moreover they were dependent on the existing government services for local knowledge. Therefore at the beginning they could achieve a considerable effect by promoting to the top people who had previously occupied comparatively junior positions. The early days of Japanese rule were a time of opportunity for the young and ambitious, especially among the Malays.

The civilian administration was in the main a facade. Such activities as education, medical services and public works were starved of funds, material and personnel. The actual work involved was improvisation rather than creative development. But in some cases it was done well; and it gave a sense of power and consequence until Japanese themselves arrived to take over. One of the effects of having local men as directors and administrators, in services in which formerly they had been assistants, was to stimulate local professional pride. The Malayan population acquired new self-confidence and the Japanese acquired a reputation for being in earnest about their pan-Asianism. Similar results developed in the non-Malay technical services.

It may be questioned how far the responsibility exercised by Malayans at this time was genuine. In some cases, particularly in the early days, there can be little doubt that it was. Senior men, whose initiative had to some extent atrophied under constant

European supervision, in conditions in which quite junior Europeans had access to confidences that were denied to them, were able for a few months to exercise genuine control. The return to subordinate positions, first under Japanese and later under British superiors, inevitably made these men feel bitter and frustrated.

There were, however, others who were given status and authority in return for political services during the campaign, but were not in effect given any real administrative work to do. The effect on them, if they were intelligent enough—as many were not—to avoid being shot by the Japanese, was to give a wholly false idea of the nature of administrative work. In essence, they merely occupied positions in which they did what they were told, and others did what they told them to do, because of the framework of a police state effectively controlled by the *kempeitai,* the Japanese military police. The difficulties of controlling clever and ambitious men were much simplified in an atmosphere in which any awkward customer would simply be executed. And the problems of drawing lines that would create the least sense of injustice and frustration were easily solved in a situation where the general environment was saturated with frustration and fear.

EFFECTS ON THE MALAYS

. . . In fostering a patriotism for Malaya within the Co-Prosperity Sphere, the Japanese fostered something that ultimately turned against them. The highly emotional cult of the Emperor did not make many converts among the Malays; but stirred up feelings that could later be transferred to Malaya, in a way which the more reserved British expressions of national feeling could never do.

An interesting by-product of guerrilla activity by the Chinese against the Japanese was the spread of the cult of invulnerability among the Malays. Every man in the rural areas was liable to have to fight or be killed. Neutrality and aloofness became impossible. These were conditions in which the cult of invulnerability naturally became popular. This cult, a survival of pre-Islamic Malay magic modified in some measure by Muslim mysticism, was quite strong among the Malays before the days of British rule, and never wholly died out even in fifty years of personal security. Under the Japanese the cult was revived among the Malay peasants, one of the leaders being Kiai Salleh, a man of peasant origins himself who wielded considerable influence and power and appears to have assisted Dato Onn in mobilising Malay peasant opinion against the Malayan Union proposals [in 1946]. . . .

Some Malays had formed a fifth column to aid the Japanese against the British. Before and after the fighting this was known as the *Kesatuan Muda Melayu* (K.M.M.), or Malay Youth Movement.

During the campaign of 1941-[4]2 it came under the control of Major Fujiwara and its members wore an F armband and were known as "F men." Other Malays, including the Sultan of Pahang and many men in important positions under the Japanese, organised an anti-Japanese movement on the side of the United Nations. In some cases the same men served in both movements; and though this may denote political incompetence it would be unjust to condemn it as mere treachery and self-interest. Certainly it is not always regarded as such among the Malays themselves.

It is a fact of considerable importance to the subsequent history of Malaya that no Malay guerrillas were trained by the British to operate against the Japanese. Both the Malay Regiment and the Malay Volunteers fought well against the Japanese. . . .

EFFECTS ON THE CHINESE

The effects of the Occupation on the Chinese were far more complex. To begin with, there was a very considerable massacre of Chinese by the invaders. So far as can be ascertained, the Japanese were concerned to kill three classes of Chinese: active supporters of Kuomintang, active Communists, and those who had fought in the Volunteer forces and not surrendered.

The [British] authorities had, immediately before the fall of Singapore, armed and trained a number of stay-behind parties behind the Japanese lines. These were composed mainly of Communists, some of whom had been serving prison sentences. They did some hard fighting against the Japanese and . . . form[ed] part of the nucleus of the . . . guerrilla forces in the jungle. The Kuomintang also organised a small guerrilla force, but this was generally admitted to be less disciplined and far less effective than the Communist force. Both groups secured a considerable measure of support from the Chinese, in spite of the fact that they certainly took reprisals against some Chinese who refused to pay.

The Chinese who had served in the Volunteers, and engaged in other acts deemed pro-British by the Japanese, were of two kinds. Some, probably a fairly small proportion, were genuinely attached to British rule, British ways and British institutions. The majority were probably actuated partly by ambition, partly by a desire to stand well with authority, partly by various other motives and inducements. Many who had worked in government service before the war returned without acute discomfort to work under the Japanese. Malays who did this probably believed that Japan now stood in the same protective relation to their States as Britain had done; Indians may have thought they were working for the liberation of India. Chinese, with no such pretext, nevertheless accepted the situation philosophically. It was merely a matter of economics. There was no other government to work for. It is unreasonable for a colonial government to expect from its subjects the attitude that a free government expects from its citizens.

Those who were genuinely pro-British in their attitude and who succeeded, by keeping out of the limelight, in escaping with their lives if not their property, expected to be rewarded for their loyalty when the long-awaited liberation arrived. When the British returned and treated all inhabitants in very much the same way they felt bitter and frustrated. It is probably this as much as anything that accounts for the intensely bitter feelings generated by any real or imagined instances of racial discrimination, such as were inevitable in a situation in which the Japanese had treated Asians in one way and Europeans in another. And it is probably this that put an end to the propaganda of loyalty to the British Empire, such as was frequently voiced before the war through bodies like the Straits Chinese British Association.

British loss of prestige as a result of military defeat is often cited as the chief cause of this change, but the break in continuity of the colonial tradition and the failure to solve the problems of the return to Malaya are probably equally important. During the Occupation there was a strong sense of comradeship in face of the common enemy between Chinese (especially of the trading class) and British internees and prisoners of war. But this attitude was quite different from the prewar attitude. When, in 1946, a group of ex-internees, in publicly thanking and rewarding a Chinese who had signally helped them in Singapore, referred to his "loyalty" the expression provoked widespread hostility among the Chinese. They felt (no doubt wrongly) that a deliberate attempt was being made to make political capital out of an act of friendship and comradeship against the enemy. . . .

Chinese leaders in turn have . . . cit[ed] as evidence of loyalty to Britain, or even to Malaya, acts of friendship to individual British prisoners or of hostility to the Japanese. This is misleading. There is plenty of evidence that the Chinese regarded the British partly as personal friends in misfortune, partly as allies against the Japanese. Loyalty in the old sense virtually disappeared in 1942, or at best in 1945. The effect of the war and the Occupation on the Chinese thus depended very much on their situation and their initial attitude.

First there were the guerrillas: the efficient and powerful three-star organisation, or Malayan People's Anti-Japanese Army, Communist-led and active against the Japanese supply lines, punishing their collaborators, and levying tithes from both willing and unwilling supporters, by any pressure that they could bring to bear. Beginning with the nucleus armed by the British just before the fall of Singapore they increased greatly in numbers as a result of Japanese brutality towards the Chinese. They were joined however by many terrorists and extortioners who had no political motives but merely robbed for a living in the chaotic economic conditions that prevailed at the time. Not all of these were brought under Communist control even by the end of the war.

To the great mass of the Chinese who survived the initial massacres, the Occupation period was one of insecurity and also of opportunity. Large fortunes were to be made, but not by those who were squeamish about legality or conventional methods of behaviour. Bribery of individual Japanese, black market deals, smuggling, and racketeering in various degrees, became the keys to success and prosperity. People became accustomed, at least in the countryside, to paying taxes to two or more authorities, and avoiding the attentions of both as far as possible. Most probably feared

the Japanese more than the guerrillas, and approved of the guerrillas more than of the Japanese. But the habits of law and order
were lost in the business sector.

Those who had served the British Government for security of
tenure and position now served the Japanese for protection from
police persecution. They were paid less than the British had paid;
and the inflation progressively reduced the purchasing power of
their earnings. The Japanese dollar fell from parity with the old
British dollar to virtually nothing, and was declared worthless
when the British returned. Hence civil servants had to supplement
their income by petty corruption, by business deals on the side or
by selling furniture and other assets to intermediaries who resold
either to Japanese or to food producers in the countryside.

A comparatively small number actively collaborated against their
own community, as procurers for the Japanese agents, for the police
and the like. A substantial proportion of the detectives for the
kempeitai were Chinese. But far more acquired a vested interest
in the disorder and insecurity of Japanese rule which brought
them wealth at the expense of the rest of society.

No one is likely to underrate the importance of the Occupation
period in stimulating guerrilla organisation among the Chinese.
But other effects may have been in the aggregate more important;
the inculcation of the habit of paying extortion money; the vast increase in bribery and irregularity of all kinds; the undermining of
the prewar respect for government and law; and the stimulation to
fantastic extremes of the tendency among the South Seas Chinese
to be steadfastly neutral on all political issues and concentrate attention on personal advancement.

EFFECTS ON THE INDIANS

The group most affected by the war and the Japanese Occupation
was the Indian community. From being depressed and uninterested
inhabitants of a political backwater, the Indians of Malaya became, in their own estimation at least, the spearhead of a movement to liberate India. For it was in Singapore that the Azad Hind
Government was set up, and it was in Malaya that most of the personnel for the Indian National Army were recruited.

Very soon after the coming of the Japanese Army, Indian Independence League branches were set up in every major centre in Malaya. Their aim was to spread propaganda, to collect funds, and to recruit and train workers and troops for a fighting movement to liberate India.

The original organizer of the movement was Major Fujiwara, a senior intelligence officer on the staff of General Yamashita. Though he had to work through interpreters he was extremely efficient in picking enthusiastic Indian personnel, and giving them enough freedom of action to convert the former Indian Associations into active political bodies. But the following up of the original enthusiasm was at first less successful. Rash Behari Bose, whom the Japanese had designated as the leader of Indian Independence, proved unpopular and unsuccessful. He was too obviously a Japanese puppet, and it is said in Malaya that his Japanese cap did more than any other one thing to alienate Indian support.

The original efforts to organise an Indian National Army fared no better. Mohan Singh, one of the first officers to desert from the British forces, and joint organiser with Akram of the first Indian National Army of 15,000 men, resigned his command in protest against three grievances, and was later put into custody. One of the points at issue was his refusal to fight without a large enough force to take independent military action. As a result of this quarrel, and also a split in the command of the Indian Independence League, the first army was disbanded.

It is important to emphasize that, though the Japanese no doubt intended the movement for Indian Independence to be merely another puppet in their pan-Asianism, this was strongly and to a limited extent successfully, resisted by the Indians themselves. There can be little doubt that the leaders felt they were using the Japanese almost as much as the Japanese were using them.

By making some concessions to Indian opinion and giving some genuine freedom of action the Japanese were able to revive the Indian National Army and use the Indian Independence League for their own purposes. The Army was reorganised under Colonel Bhonsale and a Council of Indian Colonels. The civilian organisation was given new energy by the arrival of its *Netaji*, Subhas Chandra Bose. Finally in October 1943 the Azad Hind Government was set up in Singapore.

Opinions will no doubt differ . . . on the extent to which the Indian National Army was mainly financed by extortion levied with the protection of the Japanese police state, and recruited by press-gang methods with the aid of the *kempeitai*. It is impossible for anyone with experience in interpreting Japanese propaganda to turn again to the files of the *Syonan Times* in Singapore without realising that a good deal of pressure on the wealthier Indians was prevalent. . . .

It is unwise, however, to make too much of these facts in interpreting the effects of the Indian Independence League on nationalism in Malaya. . . . People may remember their real motives for any action less than the dramatization which they made for themselves, consciously or unconsciously, to sustain their self-respect. There can be little doubt that there was a good deal of genuine Indian patriotism stirred up by Bose's oratory in a community unaccustomed to political speeches, a community out of the main current of Indian affairs and suddenly led to feel itself a vital and important element in Indian history. . . .

The Indian National Army was defeated. Its *Netaji* was killed and thousands of its men also. Their memorial built in July 1945 on the Singapore Esplanade was pulled down by other Indian troops who landed within two months. . . .

Yet echoes of the Indian National Army still linger in Malaya. The Indian community learnt the use of arms, learnt how to organise politically, and learnt some of the techniques of political bargaining. But even more important for the future was the fact that it learnt a sense of consequence. The Congress Party accepted the Indian National Army as heroes and in many parts of India they are honoured today. Whatever may be the future of the Indians in Malaya, these facts will not be easily forgotten.

26. *Effects of the Japanese Occupation in Southeast Asia*

In none of the Southeast Asian countries were the invading Japanese armies openly assisted by the national elements, although at the time stories circulated to the effect that Malays had taken up arms against the British in Malaya. In Burma no cooperation was afforded the Japanese except by a few groups of student national-ists. Even without material assistance from Southeast Asian peoples the Japanese made short work of the colonial defenders, and the extraordinary military successes of Japan did much damage to the prestige of the Western powers. The general effects of the Japanese occupation in Southeast Asia is traced in the following selection ex-tracted from Professor D. G. E. Hall, A History of South-East Asia *(Macmillan & Co., Ltd., London, 1955, pp. 688-693). Reprinted by permission.*

'Asia for the Asians' was the general theme of Japanese propa-ganda, and she sought the complete eradication of Western influ-ence and culture. To the Buddhist countries of the mainland her propaganda made much play with the fact that she also was a Bud-dhist country, although the differences between their Theravada and her Zen Buddhism of the Northern school were irreconcilable. Her relations with the Mohammedan peoples were less easy. In Indonesia she loudly proclaimed a 'Three A Movement' with three slogans: 'Japan the Leader of Asia', 'Japan the Protector of Asia', and 'Japan the Light of Asia', but it had to be abandoned for lack of support. The Japanese in Asia, like the Germans in Europe, showed a genius for alienating any people over whom they estab-lished control. In Malaya they relied on stirring up Malay hostility against the Chinese, and with some success, but they failed to arouse Malay hatred against the British, notwithstanding the extent to which their defeat had shattered their prestige.

In Burma's case practically the whole British element in the ad-ministration, and much of the Indian, escaped to India. The Bur-mese members, together with those belonging to the non-Burmese indigenous races, remained behind at their posts, as indeed they had been expected to do. The Japanese retained the administration in operation with few changes. Their method of ensuring that their requirements were fulfilled was to appoint political com-missars to work along with the civil administrators. Much of the work had to be carried on in English, since Burmese and Japanese were for the most part ignorant of each other's languages.

Much of the same thing, *mutatis mutandis*, happened to the British administration in Malaya and the Dutch in Indonesia, save that in both cases the European members of the administrative corps were interned in prison camps. In all three cases the Europeans had to be replaced by generally inadequately trained, and often hostile, Burmese, Malays and Indonesians. And as the military dominated every form of activity and knew little or nothing of civil administration, misery and confusion resulted and an inevitable deterioration of economic conditions. Everywhere the Japanese attacked those parts of the administration where the European tradition was strongest.

The police came under the direction of the Kempeitai, and probably no one will ever know the full extent of the terrorism carried on against the native populations. Thousands of Chinese were massacred soon after the surrender of Singapore, especially those who had anything to do with the China Relief Fund. . . .

There were resistance groups everywhere, for the dense jungle and mountainous areas lent themselves to this form of activity. They were often led by European officers, left behind by the retreating armies or parachuted in. In Malaya the Chinese Communists were the mainspring of the underground movement, though Kuomintang Chinese and Malays also played a part. As time went on they came to number nearly 7,000 men and women together with about 300 British, most of whom were dropped by parachute. . . . They gradually disrupted rail traffic, and in 1945 were ready to paralyse the Japanese system of communications when the British army attacked.

In Burma a Karen resistance movement led by British officers was stamped out with appalling atrocities. But a large part of the Burmese Thakin Party, disgusted by the behaviour of the Japanese, also went underground, and by the end of 1943 were leading a small but well-organized resistance movement. In their case also the Communists were the leading spirits. In French Indo-China the Viet Minh League, under the leadership of Ho Chi Minh, became the spearhead of the resistance after the collapse of a number of nationalist risings. In the last stage of the conflict they received American weapons and technical aid which enabled them to clear the Japanese out of several provinces of northern Tongking. In Cochin China Ho Chi Minh's guerrillas assisted the Resistance Committee which maintained touch with the Allies.

In Indonesia at the outset the nationalist leaders had, apparently by agreement, divided into two groups. One, headed by Sukarno and Hatta, co-operated with the Japanese as a means of furthering the nationalist cause. The other, headed by Sjahrir and Sjarifuddin, went underground to organize a resistance movement, in which they kept in touch with their comrades on the Japanese side.

In Thailand Pridi, who resigned his position as Minister of Finance when P'ibun capitulated to the Japanese, tried unsuccessfully to establish an independent government in the north. He was then made regent, and under cover of his privileged position organized an underground movement in secret touch with the Free Thai Movement in the United States and Britain. Allied forces working through his underground prepared airfields and imported arms ready for an attack on the Japanese, which never came off owing to the suddenness of their [the Japanese] collapse in 1945. . . .

In face of . . . [the growing Allied] threat the Japanese began to lose their confidence. They decided that everything must be done to win over the peoples of the occupied countries and enlist them to resist Allied attacks. Their method was to set up puppet régimes with the semblance of independence. On 1 August 1943 Burma became 'independent' under the presidency of the former premier Dr. Ba Maw, who took the title of 'Adipadi', the Pali equivalent of *Führer*. There was no talk of reviving the Constitution of 1937, and in any case real control was in the hands of Dr. Gotara Ogawa, formerly a Cabinet minister in Tokyo, who became 'Supreme Adviser' to the Burmese government. A similar régime was established in the Philippines on 15 October 1943 under Jose P. Laurel.

As Indonesia seemed unlikely to be threatened by an early Allied attack, the Japanese moved more slowly there. But the Indonesians were promised a share in their government, and in September 1943 a Central Advisory Council was established in Java under Sukarno, with Mohammed Hatta as his deputy. Advisory councils were also set up in the various residencies and cities. Sukarno's position, however, was less that of an adviser than of a mouthpiece for the interpretation and recommendation of Japanese policy to the general public. At Singapore a Malayan Consultative Council was brought into being.

But these were all mere play-acting and failed to disguise the hollowness of Japanese promises and propaganda. Of all the oc-cupied countries Burma suffered worst at the hands of the Japanese. Many of her towns had been reduced to ashes by Japanese air-raids during the invasion. Her oil-wells, mines equipment and river trans-port were destroyed by the retreating British so as to be useless to the enemy. Allied air-raids kept her railways out of action. The Japanese systematically looted the country of machinery, scientific apparatus and furniture. All her normal external markets were lost. The complete stoppage of her rice export through the failure of the Japanese to take it led to mere subsistence farming. The south suffered from a glut of rice while the north starved. Lower Burma was almost completely deprived of the cooking oil which only the dry zone could supply.

The inability of the Japanese to export Burma rice and import urgently needed consumer goods caused the greatest distress, which was further aggravated by the chaos and uncontrollable inflation caused by the Japanese currency policy. The peasantry lost a large proportion of their indispensable cattle through military requisi-tion for food and an epidemic of rinderpest. Malaria control meas-ures ceased and the people suffered heavily from the disease. There were epidemics of smallpox, cholera and bubonic plague, against which the Japanese had to take drastic preventive measures. Hence in 1944 the extremists, who had assisted the Japanese invasion and were in positions of political control, were secretly engaged in or-ganizing a nationwide Anti-Fascist People's Freedom League, which only awaited a favourable opportunity to come out openly against the oppressor.

In Malaya there was the same neglect of health measures with a consequent increase in malaria and other diseases, accompanied by a sharp rise in the death-rate. All this was particularly notice-able because the public health administration of Singapore and Malaya had been unsurpassed anywhere in Asia. The Japanese looted the hospitals of their modern up-to-date equipment and stores. The schools also were thoroughly looted and some of the native teachers executed. Famine and malnutrition in the towns were even worse than in Burma, since pre-war Malaya had imported two-thirds of its rice, and the Japanese failed to import enough from the rice-producing areas they controlled. There was also the same appalling shortage of consumer goods, and the same inflation through the uncontrolled issue of paper money. The great dredges in the European-run tin mines had been destroyed or put out of action during the British retreat in 1941-[4]2, and there had been widespread destruction of buildings and machinery on the rubber estates.

Dr. van Mook [Lieut. Governor-General of the Dutch East Indies] has summed up the effects of Japanese misrule in Indonesia in a statement which for vigour and conciseness cannot be improved upon: 'Those who suffered most were the common people. Japanese economy was frightful, Japanese administration a farce. The country had been subdivided from the beginning into three almost watertight compartments: two, Java and Sumatra, under army commanders, and a third, the rest, under the navy. But as food and other commodities became scarce even the traffic between districts and islands was prohibited in order to facilitate pillaging by the military. The system of finance consisted of a number of printing presses, turning out crude government notes; inflation acquired disastrous proportions. Trade and export production were dead, because Indonesia was cut off from the world markets[,] and Japan, her shipping going under the blows of allied submarines and aircraft, preferred to fetch the products she needed from Indo-China, a thousand miles nearer home. She remained interested only in oil, nickel and bauxite. Estates and factories rusted and decayed; plantations were uprooted to increase the food acreage; means of communication that broke down were no longer repaired; the import goods were gone or hoarded; clothing became almost unobtainable. This meant unemployment for hundreds of thousands; it meant poverty, poverty, poverty, for all but a few henchmen of the Japanese and a number of black marketeers.'

7

INDEPENDENCE AND
THE COLONIAL RECKONING

As the war turned slowly against Japan and her Axis partners, the Southeast Asian nationalists began planning for the day of liberation and for the establishment of independent regimes. In Burma the British had promised independence shortly before the collapse of Japan, and in January, 1948, the British Governor, Sir Hubert Rance, handed the instruments of sovereignty to the President of the new Burmese republic, Sao Shwe Thaik. In Malaya it was not deemed advisable to push ahead with plans for independence so rapidly, and the British, after attempting radical constitutional reform aimed at uniting all nine federated and unfederated Malay states, together with Penang and Malacca, into one union on the basis of common citizenship, were forced to shelve the measure because of Malay opposition and to propose a transitional period during which the country would prepare itself for eventual independence. This was finally achieved in August, 1957.

Elsewhere in Southeast Asia, action directed toward achieving independence was more violent. In Indonesia the two most prominent of the nationalist leaders, Dr. M. Hatta and Ir. Sukarno, who had collaborated with the Japanese as a means of securing independence for their country, seized the initiative in August, 1945, to proclaim the establishment of the new Republic of Indonesia: "We, the peoples of Indonesia, herewith proclaim the independence of Indonesia. All matters connected with the transfer of power, etc., will be carried out effectively and in the shortest possible time."

27. The Proclamation of Independence
in Indonesia

The effects of the proclamation of independence in Indonesia and the immediate reaction of the Japanese to it are described in the following selection from Dorothy Woodman, The Republic of Indonesia *(The Cresset Press, London, 1955, pp. 196-198). Reprinted by permission.*

With the proclamation of the Republic, thousands of men and women who worked secretly in resistance organizations and thousands more who had collaborated with the Japanese authorities could now show their real feelings. Civil servants, police, the army, and many organizations immediately declared their support for the Republic. Mass meetings were held in spite of the fact that the Japanese were everywhere. Leaders of demonstrations were prepared for an attack by Japanese military or police, but met no opposition. The Japanese knew that they were no longer even temporary rulers. Sukarno, who became the first President, issued an order to all civil servants to ignore orders from the Japanese; he announced that henceforth only the red-and-white flag of the Republic should be allowed to fly from all offices. The Rising Sun had set for ever. In some places a struggle took place over the flags; Japanese who had never before seen their flag hauled down made a last protest, and held out for some weeks in certain areas. Although their Government had now officially surrendered to the Allies, there were Japanese who still believed they could make a stand in Indonesia. Many of them were killed, many committed suicide. The long-pent-up feeling of Indonesians was expressed in many acts of violence; the Japanese had taught them well.

The first fortnight of the Republic, namely the period between the proclamation and the arrival of the first Allied troops, was inevitably a time of confusion. The resistance movement was strongest in Java; and it was there that the Republic was declared. News quickly spread throughout the other islands, but was generally a few days after August 17th before the red-and-white flag was flying in Sumatra and Borneo, in Celebes, the Moluccas, and Bali. But the Republic was in existence. There was no going back from President Sukarno's declaration from Pegangsaan Timur.

Two days after the proclamation of the Republic, the Preparatory Committee divided the country into eight provinces: West Java, Central Java, East Java, Sumatra, Borneo (now called Kalimantan), Celebes (now called Sulawesi), Maluku (Moluccas), and Sunda Ketjil (Lesser Sunda Islands). Governors were appointed from the local resistance leaders and local committees were set up on the same pattern as that in Djakarta.

The Japanese, taken by surprise, acted quickly. They immediately imprisoned Admiral Mayeda [who had shown sympathy towards the Indonesian nationalists] and his staff. . . . The response to the declaration of independence was so overwhelming that they decided not to go ahead with their original plan to arrest Sukarno and Hatta. Young men trained in Japanese methods of warfare refused to give up their arms and clashes were common; in many areas, Indonesians were able to defeat Japanese units and take over control. In Djakarta, the newly proclaimed Republic won the support of the masses, and the leaders of underground organizations emerged to become members of the Komita Nasional Indonesia Pusat (Central Indonesian National Committee) which took the place of the Preparatory Committee for Independence. That is, all except [the undercover Indonesian nationalist leader Sutan] Sjahrir. Sjahrir mistrusted Sukarno, fearing that he would take too indefinite a stand against the Japanese in his declaration of independence. The result was that Sjahrir and his group were not present when the proclamation was made. Sjahrir turned down an offer to serve in Sukarno's first Cabinet and made a tour of Java to judge for himself the general atmosphere. He found 'a large and strongly national front' in opposition to the now apathetic Japanese authorities, a sense of unity which 'reached greater heights' than he had imagined. Everywhere Sukarno was the popular hero and the unquestioned leader. When President Sukarno instructed all Indonesian civil servants to ignore Japanese orders, to obey the Republic of which he was the head, and to fly the red-and-white flag from all offices, the response was immediate and widespread. A people's revolution was born in the struggle of the flags. . . .

Sukarno was the symbol of the Republic. Convinced that no

other leader had mass support comparable with that which Sukarno had won during the Japanese occupation, Sjahrir returned to Dja-karta and gave his allegiance to the Republican Cabinet though he was never a member. Most of its members were men who had held high positions under the Japanese and few underground lead-ers had been appointed. This caused a great deal of dissatisfaction, especially among the students and youth who had provided the driving force of resistance. Some of them believed that certain Cabi-net members had collaborated with the Japanese as long as it suited their own purpose and then transferred their enthusiasm to the young Republic for no more laudable motives; others felt that some restriction should be placed on the powers of the President. Sjahrir shared these ideas with a number of young men who had worked with him in the underground. Together they organized a 'sort of joint executive bureau in the students' assembly hall to direct action in Batavia,' Sjahrir writes, 'and more decisions were made there than in Pegangsaan, where the Republican government assembled daily'. Finally, when the situation changed sharply with the arrival of British forces, this group round Sjahrir organized a petition to Sukarno urging that the K.N.I.P. (Central Indonesian National Committee) should be given real legislative powers jointly with the President. Hatta and Sukarno agreed to this change and in Sukarno's decree approving it, powers were delegated to a small permanently sitting body called the Working Committee, of which Sjahrir was elected Chairman. Members included Sjarifuddin (Vice-Chairman) and twelve others, most of them men with a fine record of anti-Japanese resistance. One of their first steps was the enlargement of the K.N.I.P. to 188 members fully representative of every part of the Republic. The K.N.I.P. was in fact the first Parlia-ment and the Working Committee functioned as a Cabinet.

28. Declaration of Independence of the Republic of Vietnam, 1945

The arrival of the British and Allied forces in Indonesia was soon followed by the Dutch, who attempted by armed "police action" to crush the new Indonesian Republic. These attempts came close to success, but after a long and bitter four-year struggle the Republic was formally recognized and accorded independence.

In Vietnam the nationalist leader Ho Chi Minh also seized the opportunity of the sudden collapse of the Japanese to declare the independence of the new republic from French rule. The text of the declaration is taken from A. B. Cole, Conflict in Indo-China and International Repercussions, A Documentary History, 1945-1955 *(Cornell University Press, 1956, pp. 19-21). Reprinted by permission.*

"All men are created equal. They are endowed by their Creator with certain inalienable rights, among these are Life, Liberty, and the Pursuit of Happiness."

This important statement was made in the Declaration of Independence of the United States of America in 1776. . . . The Declaration of the Rights of Man and the Citizen of the French Revolution in 1791 also states: "All men are born free and with equal rights, and must always be free and have equal rights." . . .

Nevertheless for more than eighty years, the French imperialists deceitfully raising the standard of Liberty, Equality, and Fraternity, have violated our fatherland and oppressed our fellow citizens. They have acted contrarily to the ideals of humanity and justice.

In the province of politics, they have deprived our people of every liberty.

They have enforced inhuman laws; to ruin our unity and national consciousness, they have carried out three different policies in the north, and the center and the south of Vietnam.

They have founded more prisons than schools. They have mercilessly slain our patriots; they have deluged our revolutionary areas with innocent blood. They have fettered public opinion; they have promoted illiteracy.

To weaken our race they have forced us to use their manufactured opium and alcohol.

In the province of economics, they have stripped our fellow citizens of everything they possessed, impoverishing the individual and devastating the land.

They have robbed us of our rice fields, our mines, our forests, our raw materials. They have monopolized the printing of bank-notes, the import and export trade; they have invented numbers of unlawful taxes, reducing our people, especially our country folk, to a state of extreme poverty.

They have stood in the way of our businessmen and stifled all their undertakings; they have extorted our working classes in a most savage way.

In the autumn of the year 1940, when the Japanese fascists violated Indochina's territory to get one more foothold in their fight against the Allies, the French imperialists fell on their knees and surrendered, handing over our country to the Japanese, adding Japanese fetters to the French ones. From that day on, the Vietnamese people suffered hardships yet unknown in the history of mankind. The result of this double oppression was terrific: from Quangtri to the northern border two million people were starved to death in the early months of 1945.

On the 9th of March, 1945, the French troops were disarmed by the Japanese. Once more the French either fled, or surrendered unconditionally, showing thus that not only were they incapable of "protecting" us, but that they twice sold us to the Japanese.

Yet, many times before the month of March, the Vietminh had urged the French to ally with them against the Japanese. The French colonists never answered. On the contrary, they intensified their terrorizing policy. Before taking to flight, they even killed a great number of our patriots who had been imprisoned at Yenbay and Caobang.

Nevertheless, towards the French people our fellow citizens have always manifested an attitude pervaded with toleration and humanity. Even after the Japanese putsch of March, 1945, the Vietminh have helped many Frenchmen to reach the frontier, have delivered some of them from Japanese jails, and never failed to protect their lives and properties. . . .

The whole population of Vietnam is united in common allegiance to the republican government and is linked by a common will, which is to annihilate the dark aims of the French imperialists.

We are convinced that the Allied nations which have acknowledged at Teheran and San Francisco the principles of self-determination and equality of status will not refuse to acknowledge the independence of Vietnam.

A people that has courageously opposed French domination for more than eighty years, a people that has fought by the Allies' side these last years against the fascists, such a people must be free, such a people must be independent.

For these reasons, we, members of the provisional government of Vietnam, declare to the world that Vietnam has the right to be free and independent, and has in fact become a free and independent country. We also declare that the Vietnamese people are determined to make the heaviest sacrifices to maintain its independence and its liberty.

29. Independence for Malaya

Not all the new nation states of Southeast Asia were born in conflict and revolution. In Malaya, after a long period of tutelage, the British government formally surrendered sovereignty to the new Federation at an impressive ceremony held at the Merdeka *[Freedom] Stadium, Kuala Lumpur, on August 31, 1957, at which the Duke of Gloucester, acting on behalf of the British Queen, formally handed over to the Prime Minister of the new Malayan Government the constitutional instruments granting independence. The selection is the text of the Proclamation of Independence which was read by the Malayan Prime Minister Tengku Abdul Rahman on this occasion.*

In the name of God, the Compassionate, the merciful. Praise be to God, the Lord of the Universe and may the blessings and peace of God be upon his messengers.

And Whereas the time has now arrived when the people of the Persekutuan Tanah Melayu will assume the status of a free independent and sovereign nation among the nations of the world;

And Whereas by an agreement styled the Federation of Malaya Agreement, 1957, between Her [Britannic] Majesty the Queen and Their Highnesses the Rulers of the Malay States it was agreed that the Malay States of Johore, Pahang, Negri Sembilan, Selangor, Kedah, Perlis, Kelantan, Trengganu and Perak and the former Settlements of Malacca and Penang should as from the 31st day of

August, 1957, be formed into a new Federation of States by the name of Persekutuan Tanah Melayu;

And Whereas it was further agreed between the parties to the said agreement that the Settlements of Malacca and Penang aforesaid should as from the said date cease to form part of Her Majesty's dominions and that Her Majesty should cease to exercise any sovereignty over them;

And Whereas it was further agreed by the parties aforesaid that the Federation of Malaya Agreement, 1948, and all other agreements subsisting between Her Majesty the Queen and Their Highnesses the [Malay] Rulers or any one of them immediately before the said date should be revoked as from that date and that all powers and jurisdiction of Her Majesty or of the Parliament of the United Kingdom in or in respect of the Settlements aforesaid or the Malay States or the Federation as a whole should come to an end;

And Whereas effect has been given in the Federation of Malaya Agreement, 1957, by Her Majesty the Queen, Their Highnesses the Rulers, the Parliament of the United Kingdom and the Legislatures of the Federation and of the Malay States;

And Whereas a constitution for the Government of the Persekutuan Tanah Melayu has been established as the supreme law thereof;

And Whereas by the Federal Constitution aforesaid provision is made to safeguard the rights and prerogatives of Their Highnesses the [Malay] Rulers and the fundamental rights and liberties of the people and to provide for the peaceful and orderly advancement of the Persekutuan Tanah Melayu as constitutional monarchy based on Parliamentary democracy;

And Whereas the Federal Constitution aforesaid having been approved by an Ordinance of the Federal Legislatures, by the Enactments of the Malay States and by resolutions of the Legislatures of Malacca and Penang has come into force on the 31st day of August, 1957, aforesaid;

Now in the name of God the Compassionate, the Merciful I, Tengku Abdul Rahman Putra ibni Al-Marhum Sultan Abdul Hamid Halimshah, Prime Minister of the Persekutuan Tanah Melayu, with the concurrence and approval of Their Highnesses the Rulers of the Malay States do hereby proclaim and declare on behalf of the people of the Persekutuan Tanah Melayu that as from the thirty-first day of August, nineteen hundred and fifty-seven, the Persekutuan Tanah Melayu comprising the States of Johore, Pahang, Negri Sembilan, Selangor, Kedah, Perlis, Kelantan, Trengganu, Perak, Malacca and Penang is and with God's blessing shall be for ever a sovereign democratic and independent State founded upon the principle of liberty and justice and ever seeking the welfare and happiness of its people and the maintenance of a just peace among all nations.

30. *The Colonial Balance Sheet*

The charges so forcibly leveled by Ho Chi Minh against the French colonialists in Indo-China (Selection 28) can be paralleled in the writings of other Southeast Asian nationalist leaders. Against these charges may usefully be placed the following defense of colonialism written by the late Dr. Victor Purcell, a former member of the British colonial administration in Malaya. The selection is extracted from his book, The Revolution in Southeast Asia *(Thames and Hudson, London, 1962, pp. 168-177) and reprinted by permission.*

'Colonialism' is under attack on every side, and very little is said to defend it. And even now that they have abdicated their powers to native régimes, the late 'metropolitan countries' are accused of 'neo-colonialism'—of plotting to reimpose the colonial yoke. The propaganda directed against them always depicts their behaviour in colonial times in the blackest colours, and, to the extent that it is believed, tends to poison the relations between the ex-imperial and ex-colonial peoples. Having this in mind, let us review the colonial record in Southeast Asia, in no way seeking to glorify or to extenuate, but attempting to approach at least the provisional truth in a spirit of common sense and impartiality.

It must be admitted at once that the apologist for the British Empire who wished to present the best case for it would not single out Burma as a shining example. The truth is that the British came late to Burma,[1] and were unfortunate in the situation they found and in the situation they created. Nevertheless they did bring Burma into the modern world, introduced to it a parliament, open courts of justice, and a free Press, trained Burmese in considerable numbers to administer their country, established a liberal university, and facilitated Burma's passage to independence in a way that won the unstinted praise of nationalist leaders such as U Nu.

The story of the British in Malaya[2] is in most respects a happier one than that of the British in Burma. Here they were fortunate in that they were not overtaken by the rise of a Malay nationalism,[3] impatient for independence, until towards the end of their régime, and 'Malayan' nationalism, representing Malays, Chinese, and Indians, had scarcely been born by the time that independence was granted to the Federation in 1957.[4] Thus it was that the British régime ended without bloodshed or bitterness with a peaceful transfer of power. . . .

For my part, I . . . am convinced that the British régime in Malaya served a valuable and, indeed, indispensable purpose in opening up Malaya's resources and in introducing institutions and knowledge without which the country could not have made any significant progress. . . .

Did the British investor draw an undue profit from Malaya? Taxation was fixed by the local governments, but was regulated by the Colonial Office, and it cannot be denied that the interests of 'the City' were well protected. The taxation of industry, though considerable, was not as high, perhaps, as it should have been, and as it has tended to become since independence. On the other hand, the creation of the rubber industry, a purely British innovation, was undoubtedly a permanent enrichment of the people of Malaya.

It is not necessary, however, to justify the system of private enterprise as such to make out a case for the British régime in Malaya. Economic systems everywhere are in the process of change so long as they survive, and private enterprise as it affected Malaya

[1] See Selections 13 and 17.
[2] See Selection 16.
[3] See Selection 20.
[4] See Selection 29.

was constantly being modified by legislation and even more by administrative measures. . . .

It seems to me, looking back, that it was the humanity, adaptability, and willingness to compromise which was the peculiar merit of the British régime in Malaya. Certainly the Malayan Civil Service, to which I had the honour to belong for twenty-six years, was not actuated by any profit-making motive. Even its critics admit it to have been incorrupt. It worked without stint in what its members regarded as the best interests of the country. This was true also of the medical and technical services. The first Prime Minister of an independent Malaya, Tunku Abdul Rahman, has paid public tribute to the British services on a number of occasions. . . .

The British have been charged with creating a 'plural society' in Malaya—one in which two or more communities live side by side without intermarrying and with differing standards of living—and this undoubtedly they did. But the Chinese and Indian immigrants were necessary for the development of the country, and although there was no regular control of immigration until towards the end of the trade depression of 1930-33 (and then only for economic reasons) there was no opposition to it from the Malay Rulers since the country's wealth was derived from the rubber and tin industries for which the immigrants supplied the labour. The Chinese, moreover, furnished the artisans and skilled labour for industry. The existence of a 'plural society' was and is a great obstacle to the creation of a Malayan 'nationality', but a *modus vivendi* between heterogeneous communities has been achieved elsewhere (for example Switzerland and Canada) and under the British régime the Malays, Chinese, and Indians lived harmoniously side by side.

In respect of education, the British achieved notable, if restricted, success. Elementary education in Malay was free and compulsory for all Malay boys living within a mile and a half of a Malay school, and free, but not compulsory, for all Malay girls. Education in English was not free but cheap in government and mission schools and many thousands of children were educated in that language. English was the language of law and administration except in the Unfederated States where Malay took its place, at least in theory. The larger proportion of Chinese parents, however, preferred to send their children to Chinese schools, in which 'Mandarin' was the medium of instruction, and the clash of cultures signified by these differing methods of education is one of the still unsolved problems of independent Malaya.

The most important test for a régime, however, is the preparation it made for its successor. In India, the British had admitted Indians on an equality to the Indian Civil Service for many years with the consequence that when independence came there was a competent body of Indians and Pakistanis available to carry on the administration of their respective countries. The Malayan Civil Service, a small body of about 250 officials, was composed of about four-fifths 'Europeans of pure European descent on both sides' and one-fifth to a quarter of members of the Malay aristocracy who were trained at special colleges. While it is true that in conformity with the spirit of the treaties Chinese and Indians were not admitted to the MCS, nevertheless on achieving independence the Federation possessed a nucleus of MCS Malays around which to build a new service as the European members of the Service retired and were superseded by 'Malayans'.

The consequence of British policy in Malaya from the beginning and the smooth way in which the transfer was carried out at the time of independence was that relations between the Federation Government and the ex-Colonial Power were established on a friendly footing. This (alas) was to be in sharp contrast with the relations between the Dutch and French and their respective possessions at the time of separation and afterwards.

It is a delicate matter for an ex-member of a British colonial service in Southeast Asia to criticize other European colonial régimes in that region, but the fact that both the Netherlands and France were compelled to make a complete break with Indonesia and Indochina when the separation came cannot be passed by. The reasons for it must be examined.

The Netherlands is a small country which became possessed of a large colonial empire, the greater part of it in a single region. All the Dutch colonial eggs were, so to speak, in one basket. Thus the Dutch tended to be more jealous of their rights and privileges than were the British in their much larger, more various, and much more widely distributed empire. Indonesia was considered to be so important to the Netherlands that the Dutch never envisaged that it could be separated from the Netherlands and never contemplated sharing its rule with others. In Malaya one member of the MCS in every four or five was . . . a Malay, but of the Dutch senior administrative officers in Indonesia 92 per cent were Dutchmen. . . .

The ease with which the British, Dutch, and French colonies in Southeast Asia were overrun by the Japanese did irreparable injury to the prestige of the three Metropolitan Powers.[5] Added to this, the nearly four years of occupation of Malaya and Indonesia by the Japanese, though in most ways it was a painful experience for their inhabitants, habituated them to the absence of British or Dutch authority. Both the British and Dutch had opposition to overcome on their return, but the Dutch . . . had a far more formidable task in re-establishing their control than had the British. Although forced to recognize the Indonesian Republic, they attempted (as did the French in Indochina in a similar way with regard to the Vietnam Republic) to bring it into a federal system in which they hoped to retain leadership for the Queen of the Netherlands and to exercise some sort of control as mediators between the units. Finding the Indonesians unwilling to accept their interpretation of the Linggadjati agreement, they resorted to the two unsuccessful 'police actions' which were barely disguised attempts at re-conquest. The result of these was to deepen the bitterness which already existed between the Dutch and the Indonesian Republic.

Even the long-established cultural connexion between the Netherlands and Java has almost been severed since independence. The Indonesian Government soon replaced Dutch as the second language to Indonesian Malay in its educational system by English. There were strong practical arguments in favour of this course in view of the world-wide currency of the English language, but there was also a strong emotional element in the decision. The Indonesians were still very short of text-books for their new universities, but without waiting until text-books in English became available, the universities discontinued the use of those in Dutch.

In a number of technical respects the Dutch régime of Indonesia

[5] See Selections 24, 25, and 26.

was superior to that of the British in Malaya or Burma. For example, in scientific research for rubber and agricultural production, in irrigation, and soils chemistry the Dutch gave the lead. Their administrative system was . . . excessively paternalistic, but in a number of ways—for example, rural cooperation and finance—the Dutch were the pioneers. Without any doubt they laid the foundations of modern Indonesia with great efficiency, but if their success is to be measured in terms of the gratitude felt by the Indonesians for their work, then their régime must be accounted a failure.

In Indochina, the French had even greater initial handicaps in restoring their power than had the Dutch in Indonesia. The Vichy administration set up on the fall of France had been nothing but a puppet government under the Japanese. But although the French, too, failed in their strategy, it is notable that in every successive phase of their foredoomed campaigns they enjoyed the encouragement of America and Britain. That this was the case has been the occasion of abiding resentment on the part of the Dutch, who were denied corresponding support. The political reason for this, however, is quite clear. By many American and some influential British statesmen, Indochina was looked upon as the key to 'Communist containment' . . . and in spite of all disasters it still seems to retain this position in the minds of the Americans. . . .

The French withdrawal from Indochina was, after Dien Bien Phu, as complete as that of the Dutch from Indonesia. It amounted to an abdication. . . . What influence France retained in Indochina was cultural, and this was still strong, especially in Laos. But in place of the French, it was the Americans who shored up the rickety governmental structures of South Vietnam and Laos. And yet the French, like the Dutch, had in their time performed an indispensable service in bringing the countries of the Indochinese Peninsula into the scientific and technological age.

As for the Americans, they had come late on to the colonial scene. After some initial hesitation, and deliberate 'foot-dragging' under Presidents Harding, Coolidge, and Hoover, they had facilitated the progress of the Philippines towards independence as they had promised.[6] They had developed Philippine trade greatly, but by channelling some 80 per cent of it towards the United States

[6] See Selection 19.

they had ensured that the complete economic independence of the islands from America (if it had been conceded) would be tantamount to bankruptcy. And in spite of the vast technological advance for which the Americans had been responsible, their influence was in most essential respects less profound than that of the Spanish.[7] They had, moreover, inherited an agrarian problem from the Spanish régime which they had done little to solve, except by the purchase of some large estates from the Church. Hence the agrarian insurgents, the Huxbalahaps (the 'Huks'), have been anti-American. With the continuance of the Philippines as a great American military base, the payments for the rent and the maintenance of airfields and naval ports remained an indispensable part of the Philippine revenue, and that in addition to the huge subsidies granted by America directly to the Philippine Government for economic development. Because of this abnormal situation, the Philippines stand apart from the remainder of Southeast Asia as the westernmost extension of the American Empire of the Pacific.

One final note on the colonial period may be added. In the administrative, judicial, educational, and technological spheres the achievements of the Colonial Powers were, of course, of an altogether higher order than those under the pre-colonial (and pre-scientific) 'Empires'. But in the artistic sphere, perhaps the most important, neither in India, Burma, Malaya, Indonesia, Indochina, nor the Philippines did the colonial countries leave behind them any notable architectural monuments to commemorate their régimes, although in creating pleasantly laid out cities, the French came first, the Dutch second, and the Americans and British last. There is no building of the European colonial period in South or Southeast Asia which can compare architecturally with the ruins of Angkor or Borobodur.

[7] See Selections 4 and 8.